# DROPPING THE MASK

# DROPPING THE MASK

## CONNECTING LEADERSHIP TO IDENTITY

DAPHNE Y. JEFFERSON

NEW DEGREE PRESS

COPYRIGHT © 2020 DAPHNE Y. JEFFERSON

DROPPING THE MASK

*Connecting Leadership to Identity*

ISBN      978-1-63676-320-0   *Paperback*

978-1-63676-321-7   *Kindle Ebook*

978-1-63676-322-4   *Ebook*

*To my husband, for always believing in me,*
*and to my parents, for inspiring me to dream big.*

# CONTENTS

---

# INTRODUCTION

Listen to your true self, to the inner voice that speaks of what matters most to you. Too often in our efforts to be responsive to the world around us, to take action, to get the work out the door, we grow deaf to our inner voice. We lose the ability to sense what makes our heart sing and alternatively what makes our heart sink. Listening to our inner sense of things is critical to leadership that is grounded in presence, integrity and authenticity.

−JUDY BROWN[1]

Many women spend their entire lives trying to be the next Oprah Winfrey. I hate to disappoint you, but that job has already been taken. Oprah is a unique force of nature. She was born into poverty, abused as a child, experienced teen pregnancy, and was a first-generation college graduate. She rose from news anchor and phenomenal interviewer to talk show host, and built one of the most successful media

---

1    Judy Brown, *The Art and Spirit of Leadership* (Middletown, DE: Trafford Publishing, 2012), 35.

empires in the world. You get the picture. She owns her greatness just like she owns her failures. Her honesty and vulnerability make her relatable, and her struggles remind us that with hard work and determination, you can overcome anything. Oprah's tumultuous journey forged the woman and the leader she's become. Her guiding principle is that the best way to be happy and succeed is to be the best version of you.

As I started thinking about my own leadership journey, I wondered if there is a way to help others find and embrace the best versions of themselves. My intention for this book is to take you on a voyage of discovery—a journey to your inner core. I propose that you should follow your vision and your heart to unlock the phenomenal leader who lies within you. You won't become Oprah, Michelle Obama, Sheryl Sandberg, Colin Powell, or Bill Gates. The leader you're meant to be is unique to you and represents the struggles and the triumphs that make up your specific journey. My goal is to help you be your best you.

I think of each human being as a diamond. We're all truly multifaceted creatures. Our identity is carved and shaped by our life experiences just as the diamond cutter reveals the facets of a precious stone. Just as there are no perfect diamonds, there are no perfect humans. Everyone has flaws. In fact, a perfect diamond is not necessarily the prettiest, nor is it the most valuable. As leaders, our job is to value the unique abilities of everyone on our team. Seeing each person's intrinsic value requires us to step out of our own comfort zone to meet people where they are.

We must look beyond external superficial appearances to understand and connect with how someone identifies themselves, not how others would categorize them. Stereotyping others is easy. I've heard so many times, "Oh, you're a Black woman so you must think...." There are more facets to identity than what's visible, just like the facets of a diamond.

As a teenager and young adult, I was extremely insecure. I always felt like an odd duck and an outsider. As I matured and gained more confidence in my abilities, I started to view my uniqueness as a gift. Reflecting on my early years has allowed me to focus on the question of identity, and how we, as leaders of color, can own all of the various parts of our identity. Our value depends on really understanding how to leverage everyone's unique identities to bring about change in the workplace. This understanding is the source of great leadership.

I wanted to drop the mask that hid my true identity and align what people saw on the outside with how I felt about myself on the inside. In order to do this, I spent a lot of time trying to figure out how to change my inner narrative of self-doubt and insecurity to affirmations and positive self-talk so I could build my confidence and self-esteem. I knew I had to shut down those inner voices that were telling me I wasn't good enough and replace that old narrative with a new story: I am enough.

My imperfections, my struggles, and my story all contribute to my greatness. I had to stop beating myself up for not being perfect or for thinking I had to pretend to be someone else in order for people to accept me. Once I started to embrace my new narrative, I noticed that the voice inside my head began to change. I used to have a Greek chorus of negative voices. While I still get flashes of negativity, I learned to reframe the narrative toward positivity.

I decided to write *Dropping the Mask* to pull back the curtain on the struggles of women in leadership, especially the disconnect between our public identities and the way we think of ourselves internally. I know holding up the mask is exhausting, so my book will try to help leaders reclaim their true identities by reconciling their inner and outer personas. *Dropping the Mask* will show you how to gain the confidence to be your true self and have the courage to own your story.

**DROPPING THE MASK**

Early in my career, leadership development training taught me that the best way to become a leader was to model the behaviors of others. I believe this approach fails to consider the unique personal and social identities of developing leaders. Standard leadership development programs focus on building external models for leaders to emulate. This formula does little to help emerging leaders hone their unique gifts. We learn to be like Jack Welch or some other great leader whose experiences and journey made them uniquely skilled at being themselves, which doesn't do much to help the rest of us.

Organizations invest billions of dollars each year in training programs that produce limited tangible results. In 2015, companies spent $160 billion in the United States and close to $356 billion globally on training.[2] Unfortunately, many of these leadership development efforts have yielded a poor return on investment. Barbara Kellerman, Harvard Kennedy School lecturer and founder of the Center for Public Leadership, argues that the leadership industry "has failed over its roughly forty-year history to in any major, meaningful, measurable way improve the human condition."[3] Dr. Kellerman made this assessment after a Corporate Leadership Council study found that the billions upon billions of dollars spent on leadership training has improved productivity by only 2 percent.[4]

One of the most damaging misconceptions today is that authenticity in leadership looks like someone else. Many of the "someone elses" are older white men or, on rare occasions, older white women. That person they tell you to admire is rarely a woman of color.

Women of color are projected to be the majority of all women in the United States by 2060.[5] I believe now is the time to take a different approach to developing the leaders of the future. We must move away from the cookie-cutter approach of current leadership development training and move toward approaches that embrace the diversity of today's workforce.

2    Michael Beer et al, "Why Leadership Training Fails—and What to Do About It," *Harvard Business Review* (October 2016): 50-57.

3    Rasmus Hougaard, "The Real Crisis in Leadership," *Leadership Strategy* (blog), *Forbes*, September 9, 2018.

4    Rasmus Hougaard, "When Organizations Fail to Engage Their People—The Real Crisis in Leadership," Potential Project International, accessed August 16, 2020.

5    Catalyst, "Quick Take: Women of Color in the United States," March 19, 2020, accessed May 23, 2020.

Authentic leadership doesn't look like anyone else but you, and your leadership style is an amalgamation of all of the unique experiences that define who you are.

## INTERNAL DEVELOPMENT = OWNING YOUR IDENTITY

I found several promising starting points for leadership training programs through research and my own experiences. For example, McKinsey & Company, one of the world's leading management consulting firms, conducted research that suggests the best way to develop leaders is to engage the whole person by embracing their unique identity and working to uncover unconscious bias.[6] Recommendations from Catalyst, a global nonprofit focused on building workplaces that work for women, include increasing mentoring opportunities for women and people of color, as well as changing hiring and promoting practices to eliminate unconscious bias.[7]

Every leader, at some point in their career, will face the inclination to change who they are to fit into someone else's version of a good leader. The decision you make in this situation could profoundly affect your career and your ability to look yourself in the mirror. A dysfunctional boss triggered this situation for me. I remember the feeling of dread as I approached my boss's office. I can still feel the tension in my shoulders and the tightness in my chest that happened every time I met with her. She was the poster child for the toxic leader. She would have outbursts and bully us in our

---

6   Rachel Thomas et al, "Women in The Workplace 2019," McKinsey & Company and LeanIn.Org..

7   Nancy Carter and Christine Silva, "Mentoring: Necessary but Insufficient for Advancement," Catalyst, Inc. December 6, 2010.

weekly senior staff meetings. The only upside of this particular meeting was that I was berated in private. Her message to me was "You're too nice. Your people like you too much." I sat in stunned silence for a moment. I wondered when being nice and treating people with respect had become a leadership failing.

As I left my boss's office, I had moment of clarity. I realized I had a choice: I was free to pick my own style of leadership. I could be the stereotypical dictatorial hard-ass who drives people to exhaustion, or I could be the kind of leader who respects and values the team. I chose my own way. After all, my way had taken me from being an entry-level payroll clerk to being a member of the Senior Executive Service, the highest career leadership level of federal government.

After that meeting, I decided I needed to leave my job and find an environment and culture that aligned with my values. Walking away from work that fulfilled me and a team that I loved wasn't easy, but I refused to allow someone else to impose their leadership style on me.

My goal is to help you own your leadership identity, learn to harness your authentic self, and understand how to support your team members in unlocking their unique abilities. Throughout this book, we will explore my top seven attributes for wholehearted leadership:

- Self-awareness
- Compassion
- Confidence
- Character

- Optimism
- Courage
- Agility

The purpose of this book is to help emerging leaders of color successfully navigate the challenges of leadership, but others can also benefit from it. Senior leaders and executives of diverse organizations can gain insights into the best practices for supporting those whom they lead and mentor. Leadership and executive coaches will also learn practices that can help their clients find the courage to let their true personal identity shine.

I felt compelled to write this book because my leadership journey has been challenging and I wish I had had a guide to show me how to avoid certain pitfalls. Some of the mistakes I made were necessary for my growth. Others could've derailed me had I not been equipped with grit and stubbornness. I want to leave a trail of breadcrumbs for others to follow on their journey through the wilderness in search of their true identities.

# PART ONE

# THE ROOTS OF LEADERSHIP

# CHAPTER 1

# THE JOURNEY TO LEADERSHIP

———

True heroism is remarkably sober, very undramatic. It is not the urge to surpass all others at whatever cost, but the urge to serve others at whatever cost.

—ARTHUR ASHE[8]

**FOLLOW THE YELLOW BRICK ROAD**

I decided to explore the history of leadership through the frame of one of my favorite childhood movies, *The Wizard of Oz*, in hopes of coming up with an easily digestible approach to the question, "What is leadership?"

———

8   "Arthur Ashe Biography," The Biography.com, last modified June 29, 2020.

*The Wizard of Oz* is a 1939 musical starring the late Judy Garland. She plays Dorothy Gale, a Kansas farm girl who dreams of finding a place "somewhere over the rainbow" for herself and her dog. The film is an adaptation of L. Frank Baum's children's fantasy novel, *The Wonderful Wizard of Oz*. The Library of Congress lists *The Wizard of Oz* as the most seen film in history.[9]

I remember the first time I saw *The Wizard of Oz*. As an impressionable kindergartener, I felt like I was on a magical journey with Dorothy, the Tin Man, the Cowardly Lion, the Scarecrow, and little Toto, too. I sat on the floor two feet away from the television and cried when the Wizard flew away in the balloon without Dorothy. I thought the poor girl could never go home. I couldn't watch any more of the movie and went to bed with seeing the ending.

**IN SEARCH OF A GREAT MAN**
Literary scholar Joseph Campbell outlines the stages of a hero's journey in his book, *The Hero with a Thousand Faces*. He writes, "A hero ventures forth from the world of common day into a region of supernatural wonder: fabulous forces are there encountered and a decisive victory is won: the hero comes back from this mysterious adventure with the power to bestow boons on his fellow man."[10] This description has remained the common format for stories that involve a hero or heroine who goes on an adventure or

---

9    "The Wizard of Oz: An American Fairy Tale - To See the Wizard Oz on Stage and Film," Library of Congress, December 15, 2010.
10   Joseph Campbell, *The Hero with a Thousand Faces* (Princeton: Princeton University Press, 2004).

quest: they face adversity, defeat their foe, and undergo a significant transformation.

The first part of *The Wizard of Oz* is filmed in black and white; however, once a tornado rips Dorothy's house from its foundation and deposits it in the world of Oz, colors fill the screen. The plot progresses as follows:

Dorothy's house lands on top of the Wicked Witch of the East, killing her. The witch's sister, the Wicked Witch of the West, threatens revenge on Dorothy and her little dog, Toto. Glinda the Good Witch intervenes by giving Dorothy the dead witch's magical ruby slippers. Since she doesn't have the power to send Dorothy home, Glinda tells the little girl to find the Wizard of Oz in the Emerald City, as he's the only one who can help her get back to Kansas. This is the beginning of the hero's journey for Dorothy Gale.

The hero's journey to find the meaning of leadership dates back to the mid-1800s, when the prevailing idea viewed leaders as heroic figures. From this idea, Thomas Carlyle coined the Great Man Theory in 1840: leaders are born and not made. He specifically chose the words "great man" because at the time, leadership was viewed as a masculine endeavor.[11]

I guess Thomas Carlyle forgot about great woman leaders like Cleopatra, Catherine the Great, and Queen Victoria. Marie Curie certainly didn't let gender stereotypes of the early nineteenth century stand in the way of achieving her

---

11  Thomas Carlyle, *On Heroes, Hero-worship and the Heroic in History* (London: Chapman and Hall, 1841).

goals. She was the first woman to win a Nobel Prize and is the only person—man or woman—to receive two Nobel Prizes in different scientific fields.[12] Dr. Curie said, "Nothing in life is to be feared, it is only to be understood."[13] Dr. Curie used her scientific gifts to establish an oncology hospital for women, proving gender has nothing to do with great leadership.

## AND A LITTLE CHILD SHALL LEAD THEM

Dorothy Gale meets the Scarecrow, the Tin Man, and the Cowardly Lion while traveling along the Yellow Brick Road to the Emerald City. Each of these companions is on their own personal quest—the Scarecrow to find a brain, the Tin Man to find a heart, and the Cowardly Lion to find courage. On the surface, Dorothy's goal is to get back to Kansas, but I believe she's also on her own quest to find the confidence to take charge of her life.

Just like Dorothy and her companions, researchers in the 1930s and 1940s set out to identify the leadership styles needed to be an effective leader. In 1939, psychologist Kurt Lewin's study of a group of schoolchildren helped define leadership styles for decision-making that we still use today. In Lewin's study, children were assigned to one of three types of leadership groups: authoritarian, democratic, or laissez-faire.

Authoritarian leaders provide clear expectations for what, when, and how tasks need to be done. The leader makes the

---

12   "Marie Curie – Biographical," The Nobel Prize, accessed August 18, 2020.
13   "Marie Curie the Scientist," MarieCurie.org, accessed August 18, 2020.

decisions with little to no input from the group. Authoritarian leadership may be appropriate for situations that require quick, decisive action; however, overuse of this style can be controlling, bossy, and dictatorial.

Democratic or participative leaders make decisions, offer guidance, and encourage input from other group members. Even though this type of leader has the final say in decisions, team members feel committed and valued.

Laissez-faire or delegative leaders leave decision-making to the group while offering little to no guidance. This style of leadership may work for a team of highly qualified experts, but it frequently results in role confusion and a lack of personal responsibility.

In this study, researchers observed how each of these three leadership styles affected the children's behaviors as they completed an arts and crafts project. The researchers found that democratic leadership tended to be the most effective at inspiring followers to perform well.[14]

## TRAIT THEORY: THE "EXTROVERT IDEAL"

Dorothy's band of travelers went off in search of what they believed was lacking in their personalities. The Scarecrow wanted a great intellect, the Tin Man wanted empathy, and The Cowardly Lion wanted courage. They believed these traits would make them great.

---

14   Kendra Cherry, "The Eight Major Theories of Leadership," accessed May 17, 2020.

People in the early 1900s believed great leaders possessed certain traits that separated them from non-leaders. However, in 1948, Ralph Stogdill surveyed the previous twenty-five years of research. In "Personal Factors Associated with Leadership: A Survey of the Literature," Stogdill concluded, "A person does not become a leader by virtue of the possession of some combination of traits."[15] This groundbreaking study began a shift away from believing leaders have intrinsic traits or personality characteristics such as charisma and extroversion; instead, one can cultivate desirable leadership qualities. The Scarecrow, the Tin Man, and the Cowardly Lion would probably add intelligence, empathy, and courage to the list of desirable leadership traits.

Susan Cain, former Wall Street attorney, introvert, and author of *Quiet: The Power of Introverts in a World That Can't Stop Talking*, says the "Extrovert Ideal"—"the omnipresent belief that the ideal self is gregarious, alpha and comfortable in the spotlight"—dominates Western culture.[16] She goes on to say that this view of leadership is based on the Greco-Roman ideal that praises oratory skills, favors the man of action over the man of contemplation, and views "introversion as being between a disappointment and pathology."[17] By contrast, traditional, pre-Americanized Asian culture was more inclined to value reticence and caution.[18] They might have been on to something. People such as Rosa Parks, Sir

---

15    Ralph Stogdill, "Personal Factors Associated with Leadership: A Survey of the Literature," *Journal of Psychology*, (1948): 25, 35–71.

16    Susan Cain, *Quiet: The Power of Introverts in a World That Can't Stop Talking* (New York: Broadway Books, 2013), 4-5.

17    Cain, *Quiet*, 29-30.

18    Cain, *Quiet*, 190-192.

Isaac Newton, Albert Einstein, Steven Spielberg, J.K. Rowling, Charles Schulz, Steve Wozniak, W.B. Yeats, and Eleanor Roosevelt all demonstrate that introverts can flourish in a world dominated by extroverts.

## BEHAVIORAL THEORY: NATURE VS. NURTURE

In the twenty-year period between 1950 to 1970, researchers shifted their attention away from characteristics and started to study the specific behaviors of leaders.[19] The underlying assumption was that leaders can be made rather than born and that successful leadership can be learned. This shift in thinking opened the door for leadership development instead of exclusively choosing leaders based on assessments, which shifted focus from the leader's internal personality traits to their external manifestations of leadership. Learning and observation are the cornerstones of this approach to leadership.[20]

An old proverb says that experience is the best teacher. Dorothy and her merry band had many experiences—both beautiful and terrifying—on their journey to see the Wizard. You could say that the Yellow Brick Road was their master class in leadership development; each new obstacle, from the poppy field to the flying monkeys, helped each member of the team uncover the traits they most wanted to possess.

The main contribution of the behavioral approach to leadership is the exploration of two very different kinds of leaders:

---

19   Gene Early, "A Short History of Leadership Theories," accessed May 14, 2020.

20   Early, "A Short History of Leadership Theories."

leaders who focus on work and leaders who focus on people. In *The Wizard of Oz*, the Wicked Witch of the West represents the first type of leader with her single-minded focus on taking back the ruby slippers, and Glinda represents the second type with her caring leadership of the munchkins.

## PARTICIPATIVE LEADERSHIP

In the 1950s, Rensis Likert conducted a study at the University of Michigan that set out to define the behaviors of effective leadership. Likert, a social scientist best known for developing a measurement for attitudes called the Likert Scale, introduced the concept of participative management. In his study, he proposed another type of leadership besides the task-oriented leaders who are primarily focused on the work and people-oriented leaders who are primarily focused on the people: participative leadership.[21] Participative leaders consult their entire team when creating systems and methods for achieving the team's goals.

If the Wicked Witch is task-oriented and Glinda is people-oriented, then Dorothy is a participative leader. She brings out each team member's strengths and recognizes that everyone has a valuable part to play in getting to Oz.

## SITUATIONAL LEADERSHIP

Danial Goleman is a best-selling author and leadership expert whose book, *Emotional Intelligence*, stayed on The

---

21 *Encyclopedia Brittanica Online*, s.v. "Rensis Likert," accessed May 17, 2020.

New York Times Best Sellers list for a year and a half and has been translated into forty languages. In 1995, he published game-changing research in which he developed a six-category theory of situational leadership that allowed for a deeper understanding of leadership. The six leadership styles within his model are coaching, pacesetting, democratic, affiliative, authoritative, and coercive. The effectiveness of each style is dependent on the situation or environment of the organization.[22] Goleman likened the six leadership styles to a golfer selecting different clubs to successfully navigate the changing terrain of a golf course. He wrote, "The pro 'senses' the challenge ahead, swiftly pulls out the right tool, and elegantly puts it to work."[23] One size does not fit all, and great leaders seamlessly adjust their styles to suit the situation.

## SERVANT LEADERSHIP

Robert Greenleaf began his thirty-eight-year career as an engineer with AT&T in 1926 when it was one of the largest corporations in the world. He wanted to work for a large company after a teacher had convinced him that large institutions didn't properly serve society. Greenleaf made it his mission to have a career of "quiet influence" from inside a big corporation. He quickly progressed at AT&T. He participated in its first management training program and created the world's first corporate assessment center. He fought for equity by promoting the first women and African Americans to non-menial positions within the company, and he started

---

22  Daniel Goleman, Richard E. Boyatzis, and Annie McKee, *Primal Leadership: Realizing the Power of Emotional Intelligence* (Boston: Harvard Business School Press, 2002), 55.

23  Goleman et al, *Primal Leadership*, 54.

a program that exposed up-and-coming leaders to the wider implications of corporate decisions.[24]

Greenleaf published his influential essay, "The Servant as Leader," in 1970 and later released it in his book of essays, *Servant Leadership: A Journey Into the Nature of Legitimate Power & Greatness*. This essay was more of a philosophy than a leadership theory; as Greenleaf wrote, "The servant-leader is servant first, it begins with a natural feeling that one wants to serve, to serve first, as opposed to, wanting power, influence, fame, or wealth."[25] A servant leader puts the needs of their followers first and possesses characteristics such as listening, persuasion, access to intuition and foresight, use of language, and pragmatic measurements of outcomes.[26]

## TRANSFORMATIONAL LEADERSHIP THEORY

Transformational leadership has emerged as one of the most important approaches for understanding and influencing employee effectiveness. The cornerstone of this approach is the belief that transformational leaders inspire employees to greater levels of motivation and performance through connections formed between leaders and their followers. According to this theory, helping each group member reach their fullest potential is just as important as the overall performance of the group.[27]

---

24 Don Frick, "Robert K. Greenleaf: A Short Biography," accessed August 24, 2020.

25 Ibid.

26 Robert Greenleaf, *Servant Leadership: A Journey into the Nature of Legitimate Power and Greatness* (New York: Paulist Press, 1991).

27 George Allen et al, "The Role of Servant Leadership and Transformational Leadership in Academic Pharmacy," *American Journal of Pharmaceutical Education* 80, (2016), 113.

Leadership expert and presidential biographer James Mac-Gregor Burns initially introduced the theory of transformational leadership. According to Burns, "The result of transforming leadership is a relationship of mutual stimulation and elevation that converts followers into leaders and may convert leaders into moral agents."[28] Through the strength of their vision and personality, transformational leaders are able to inspire followers to change their expectations, perceptions, and motivations in order to work toward common goals.

Researcher Bernard M. Bass expanded on Burns's ideas and developed Bass's Transformational Leadership Theory in 1979. Bass's theory states that transformational leadership is based on the impact the leader has on their followers. Transformational leaders garner trust, respect, and admiration from their followers.[29]

## OFF TO SEE THE WIZARD

Each of the characters who set off to find the Wizard of Oz transformed along the way, and their inherent leadership traits surfaced as the team made its way down the Yellow Brick Road. Their experiences taught the group to rely on each other; together, they accomplished something that initially seemed impossible: making it to the Emerald City.

---

28  James Burns, Leadership (New York: Harper & Row, 1978).
29  Bernard Bass, "From Transactional to Transformational Leadership: Learning to Share the Vision," *Organizational Dynamics*, 18 no.3 (1990), 19–31.

My journey down the Yellow Brick Road of leadership started in Atlanta, Georgia, in the 1980s. My first real job was payroll clerk for the Federal Aviation Administration (FAA). My goal was just to get my foot in the door with the federal government and work my way up from the bottom. So, I accepted the job even though it would barely pay enough to cover my rent and other essentials.

My first day on the job was surreal. I raised my hand to take the oath of office, committing to "protect and defend the Constitution against all enemies, both foreign and domestic." It seemed like a heavy burden to place on such a low-level employee. Since then, I have raised my hand to pledge that same oath every time I was promoted and have administered it to new employees dozens of times in my career. To this day, the weight of my responsibility to protect and defend the Constitution is an unshakable part of my identity.

When I started the job in payroll, I was one of the youngest people in the office. Within three months of starting, the FAA's regional payroll operations underwent a major systems transformation and added about ten thousand additional payroll accounts. The consolidations and transformation of outdated processes and technology proved to be too much for most of the older, more senior women in the office. The woman tasked with training me said, "I'm too old for this! You young folks can have it." The following week, she decided that she should retire, and many of her contemporaries headed out the door with her. We went from a staff of twelve payroll clerks down to three junior staff. All of a sudden, I had become one of the most senior payroll clerks in the office.

The old expression of drinking from a fire hose seems mild compared to the pressure I experienced while rebuilding the payroll system and ensuring that over twenty thousand employees were paid correctly and on time. That whirlwind was the most challenging yet rewarding three years of my career, and they taught me a lot of what I know about leadership. I learned how to manage transitions, think strategically in order to realize the organization's vision, and create order out of chaos.

One of the most important lessons I learned from that time is that leadership doesn't need a fancy title or a big office; you can lead from wherever you are. My core values of leadership that grew out of my time as a payroll clerk are self-awareness, compassion, confidence, character optimism, courage, and agility. These are what drive me as I continue my journey down the Yellow Brick Road of leadership.

My start in payroll allowed me to gain the skills and the confidence that took me from starting at the bottom level of the FAA to becoming an air traffic controller to working on Capitol Hill to working in the CFO's office at NASA to running a federal regulatory agency. There have been many ups and downs since those early days, but I'm eternally grateful for the experiences I've gained.

In some ways, I'm a lot like Dorothy who started down the Yellow Brick Road searching for her home and a sense of belonging; as a leader, I'm always trying to foster a sense of belonging and acceptance within my organization. Dorothy recognized the strengths and accepted the identities of her band of fellow travelers. She believed in her team and trusted that each of them had everything they needed to be successful. As Glinda the Good Witch said, "You've always had the power, my dear—you just had to learn it for yourself."[30] She brought out their best and led them to a happy ending. Just like Dorothy, I know leadership requires trust, having the courage to take risks, and supporting others along the way.

## THE TAKEAWAY

Our trip down the Yellow Brick Road of leadership theory laid a foundation so you can have a framework to understand your own leadership identity. Leadership theories can provide a language to help us define and refine who we are as leaders.

While *The Wizard of Oz* captivated me as a child, I now see so many leadership lessons on display in the film. Dorothy's ride inside the tornado reminds me of the turbulence of today's chaotic work environment. Market volatility, climate change, and global conflicts all contribute to a sense of uncertainty. Glinda's instructions to go see the Wizard was as vague as your boss saying, "You'll know it when you find it."

Dorothy's traveling companions provide a lesson in group dynamics. They're each searching for something, and Dorothy, as the de facto leader, has to manage their different talents and temperaments to survive the dangerous trip to find the Wizard. Under pressure, each character summons the skills and courage needed to protect their colleagues. In

---

30  Judy Garland, et al, *The Wizard of Oz,* (Hollywood, CA: Metro Goldwyn Mayer, 193.

the end, they learn to trust and support each other, no matter the obstacles.

Years later, I finally watched the end of the film. Spoiler alert: Dorothy makes it home. After all these years, the underlying message in *The Wizard of Oz*—that each of us has everything we need inside if we can trust ourselves enough to try—still moves me. This group of strangers started their hero's journey in search of a Great Man, but their struggles and triumphs along the way ended up being exactly what they had needed the whole time. They found that courage, confidence, and strength look different for each of us, but we all possess them if we're willing to believe in ourselves.

# CHAPTER 2

# THE ROOTS OF LEADERSHIP

—

Dreams do come true, but not without the help of others, a good education, a strong work ethic, and the courage to lean in.

—URSULA BURNS[31]

Growing up couldn't have been easy for Ursula Burns. She was raised by a single mother in a New York City housing project. Few expected much from the bright little girl with big dreams and no money, but that little girl grew up to become the first African American woman CEO of a Fortune 500 company. Ursula's leadership evolved over her thirty-five-year career at Xerox, starting as an intern and ending as the chairman of the board.

---

31   "Ursula Burns," Stories, LeanIn, accessed October 5, 2020.

Ursula Burns brings her unique identities into the workplace. She describes her authentic style of leadership as "missionary," meaning that she unites, spreads the message, remains loyal, and cares deeply about people.[32]

Women like Ursula are changing the way we think of leaders as the theory and practice of leadership continues to evolve. Leadership traits we once valued may not work today. The current leadership model is moving away from valuing traits typically associated with men. Sociology professor Crystal Hoyt wrote, "Although people often associate primarily masculine traits such as aggressiveness and dominance with leadership, effective leadership actually requires an androgynous combination of feminine and masculine traits."[33]

Early in my career, I didn't see any leaders who looked like me. I spent ten years with the FAA before I saw an African American manager. Fortunately, he took me under his wing and mentored me; up until that point, all of my mentors were white men. Another five years passed before I personally met a woman of color in a senior leadership role, but I was fortunate to have women of color like Ursula Burns who served as my role models for succeeding in corporate America.

Despite the leadership styles of my role models, the foundation of my leadership identity was my personal history. My

---

32  "Ursula Burns Inspires," (lecture, Carnegie Mellon University Tepper School of Business, Pittsburg, PA, October 14, 2019).

33  Crystal Hoyt, "Women, Men, and Leadership: Exploring the Gender Gap at the Top," *Social and Personality Psychology Compass* no. 4 (July 2010): 484–498.

life experiences, ethnicity, and family history play a major role in who I am as a leader. Women and leaders of color need to look to our own culturally influenced traits and behaviors as a guide to finding our authentic voice. The starting point for this exploration begins with those pieces of our identity that have helped us build the most important ingredient of great leadership: emotional intelligence (EQ).

## THE WISDOM OF THE ELDERS

My most important lessons about leadership didn't come from school or leadership development seminars. Instead, they came from my family in the form of lessons passed down from my grandparents to my parents to my siblings and me. Those leadership lessons were primarily about relationships. Isn't fostering positive and productive relationships what being a great leader is all about?

I'm the product of a close-knit family. We grew up having Sunday dinners at my paternal grandparents' house and spending summers at the beach with my maternal grandmother. My paternal grandfather, Pop, left his home in rural Georgia at the age of twelve to support his mother and three sisters. He had less than a sixth grade education, but he was determined to make enough money to send home to his family. He found factory work in Jacksonville, Florida, and eventually saved enough to buy a house for his mother and sisters. As an adult, Pop was a Pullman porter who worked on the railroad and ran a contract painting business on his off days. He retired from the railroad when he was sixty-six years old and kept his business going until he finally retired in his early eighties.

Margaret, my paternal grandmother, was seventeen years old when her mother died, leaving her to raise her younger siblings on her own. She did domestic work to provide for her family. My grandparents fell in love and got married in the early 1930s, and shortly after that, my father was born. While my grandparents struggled to take care of their growing family, World War II began ramping up. Pop joined the railroad and spent most of the war ferrying troops across the country. After the war, he spent the next thirty years working six days a week to provide for his family and to ensure his children got an education. When my grandmother later became a licensed beautician, Pop built a shop for her at the back of the house. Although he never had the chance to finish school, Pop made sure his children went to college. In fact, both of his children became teachers and Pop was in the audience when they received their master's degrees in education.

Pearl, my maternal grandmother, grew up in a poor, rural town in central Georgia. She was an unwed single mother with two children when she opened a restaurant in Jacksonville Beach, Florida. Segregated conditions of the 1940s and '50s barred African Americans from most of the schools and businesses in Florida. My mother had to take an hourlong city bus ride from Jacksonville Beach to get to the one Black high school in downtown Jacksonville, even though there was an all-white school in walking distance from her house. My grandmother was an astute businesswoman despite never graduating from high school. She worked seven days a week to provide for her children's education. My mother was the first person in her family to graduate from high school and the first to attend college.

My parents met in high school and started dating their freshman year of college at Florida A&M College, now Florida A&M

University. My father tells the story of the night they both arrived at the Tallahassee, Florida, train station for the start of freshman year. He said, "I thought your mother had money because she was the only person I ever met who had their own bank account and a matching set of luggage." My parents worked hard to provide their children with structure, discipline, and most of all, love. Growing up, I noticed all of the hard work and sacrifices my grandparents and parents made.

We often had family gatherings, and they were always boisterous and educational. Weekly Monday night card games for the adults meant the house would be filled with great food and the sound of my grandfather slapping the table when he had a winning hand. When I was little, I would hide under a table or in the next room, eavesdropping on the conversation. I learned about the world, politics, religion, and leadership. No one ever used words like "leadership," "entrepreneurship," "emotional intelligence," or "customer service," but they each taught me how to be a leader in their own ways.

## LEADERSHIP LESSONS FROM THE KITCHEN TABLE

My grandparents taught me the value of hard work, education, and attention to detail. They demonstrated that there's dignity in every task, no matter how small. The most important lesson I learned from them was that everyone needs to take care of their family. In the workplace, the team is the family, and the most important job for leaders is recognizing and supporting the individuals on your team.

From my parents, I learned to be gracious, compassionate, and fair, to listen more and talk less, and to lead with my heart. For as long as I can remember, my father always said, "Treat everyone in your office with respect, whether it's the janitor or the CEO."

My parents also showed me how to work hard and constantly learn new skills. My mom showed me how to be loving, kind, generous, and self-sufficient. My dad taught me how to tie my shoes and how to shine them, a lesson he learned from his father. He said, "You can tell a lot about a person by the condition of their shoes." He wasn't talking about how much money a person spent or their designer label—he meant how well they cared for their possessions. He taught us that the small details are important and indicate how someone will handle the big things in life.

I gained confidence from having a strong support structure behind me. I learned that failure isn't fatal. My family told me that "not trying hard enough or never taking risks is worse than failure." As leaders, our mission should be cultivating an environment where our team is willing to risk failure in order to innovate. They need to trust their leader enough to fail forward. That's what I learned all those years ago sitting around the family table.

## CONNECTED LEADERSHIP

Gifted leadership occurs where heart and head—
feeling and thought—meet.

–PRIMAL LEADERSHIP[34]

---

34  Daniel Goleman, Richard E Boyatzis, and Annie McKee, *Primal Leadership: Learning to Lead with Emotional Intelligence* (Boston, MA: Harvard Business School Press, 2004), 26.

Poet Maya Angelou once said, "People will forget what you said and what you did, but they will never forget how you made them feel."[35] Intellect and technical skills are frequently the entry point into a management position, but connections, relationships, and emotional competency are the keys to effective leadership. The Center for Creative Leadership reported that 75 percent of careers are derailed for reasons related to emotional incompetency. Those incompetencies included the inability to handle interpersonal problems, unsatisfactory team leadership during times of difficulty or conflict, and the inability to adapt to change or elicit trust.[36]

One of the most important differentiators between good leaders and great leaders is emotional intelligence. Some markers of EQ include the ability to correctly distinguish between and label different emotions and to use emotional information to guide thinking and behavior. Without emotional intelligence, influencing the behavior of others is difficult.[37]

Psychologists Peter Salovey and John Mayer published their landmark article "Emotional Intelligence" in 1990. They defined emotional intelligence as "the ability to monitor one's own and others' feelings and emotions, to discriminate among them, and to use this information to guide one's thinking and actions."[38] Emotional intelligence origi-

---

35  Rachel Chang, "19 Inspirational Maya Angelou Quotes," Biography, accessed August 24, 2020.

36  Jean Leslie and Michael Peterson, *The Benchmarks Sourcebook Three Decades of Related Research* (Greensboro, NC: CCL Press, 2011).

37  John Mayer, Peter Salovey, and David R. Caruso, "Emotional Intelligence," *American Psychologist* 503 (September 2008): 503–517.

38  Peter Salovey and John D. Mayer, "Emotional Intelligence," *Imagination, Cognition and Personality* 9 no. 3 (March 1990): 185–211.

nates in the neurotransmitters of the brain's limbic system, which governs feelings, impulses, and drives. Research indicates that the limbic system learns best through motivation, extended practice, and feedback.[39]

In 1995, the concept of emotional intelligence gained widespread acceptance after psychologist and journalist Daniel Goleman published his book *Emotional Intelligence: Why It Can Matter More Than IQ*. Goleman found that the top 10 percent of performers in the workplace displayed superior competencies in emotional intelligence. He wrote, "Capabilities like self-confidence and initiative; bouncing back from setbacks and staying cool under stress; empathy and powerful communication, collaboration; and teamwork all make for better business results."[40]

Goleman's model of emotional intelligence is comprised of four domains: self-awareness, self-management, social awareness, and relationship management. Self-awareness is the ability to know how you're feeling and why, as well as how those feelings help or hurt what you're trying to accomplish. Self-management is the ability to keep disruptive emotions and impulses under control. Social awareness indicates one's ability to accurately read and interpret other people's emotions, often through nonverbal cues. Relationship management allows leaders to act in ways that motivate, inspire, and harmonize with others and form important relationships.[41]

---

39   Daniel Goleman, *Emotional Intelligence: Why It Can Matter More Than IQ* (New York: Bantam Books, 1995).

40   Ibid.

41   Goleman, Boyatzis and McKee, *Primal Leadership,* 39.

TalentSmart, a company that provides emotional intelligence products and services to more than 75 percent of the Fortune 500 companies, tested EQ alongside thirty-three other important workplace skills. The researchers found that EQ is the strongest predictor of performance in 58 percent of all job types. The study found that 90 percent of top performers have a high EQ, while just 20 percent of bottom performers have a high EQ. In addition, their research has found that people with a high degree of EQ make an average of $29,000 more per year than people with a low degree of EQ.[42]

Emotional intelligence is absolutely crucial as we struggle to maintain our composure in today's high-pressure, fast-paced work environments in which stress is common. Our brains react to psychological threats in the same way they would to a physical threat, so leaders' guarding against emotional triggers and outbursts by developing emotional intelligence is vitally important.

Daniel Goleman tweeted, "The top 5 workplace amygdala triggers in the workplace: lack of respect, unfair treatment, being unappreciated, not being heard, unrealistic deadlines."[43] Think about a time when you had to respond to a last-minute request at 5:00 p.m. on the Friday before a major holiday weekend. Without emotional intelligence, someone could easily crumble under this pressure.

---

42  "About Emotional Intelligence," TalentSmart, accessed June 10, 2020.

43  Daniel Goleman (@DanielGolemanEI), Daniel Goleman. "Top 5 amygdala triggers in the workplace: lack of respect, unfair treatment, being unappreciated, not being heard, unrealistic deadlines," Twitter, 10:13 a.m., December 15, 2016.

## GET UP ON THE BALCONY

"The practice of leadership, like the practice of medicine, involves two core processes: diagnosis first and then action," said Ronald Heifetz, the founder of the Center for Public Leadership at Harvard Kennedy School.[44] He coined the phrase "getting on the balcony" as a metaphor for gaining a distanced perspective in order to spot patterns and see the larger picture. Leaders must be able to identify struggles over values and power, recognize patterns of work avoidance, and watch for functional and dysfunctional reactions to change.[45]

Heifetz believes that leadership requires sacrifice and dedication, but the rewards that come from helping others succeed outweigh the heavy emotional toll of leadership. Leaders need to seamlessly move from the strategic "balcony" to the inner chamber of self-reflection. Too much time in either place can derail a leader. Heifetz said, "The hard truth is that it is not possible to know the rewards and joys of leadership without experiencing the pain as well."[46] While this is true, I personally find that the joys and rewards of helping others reach their fullest potential far outweigh the sacrifice of leadership.

Great leaders must be agile and balance between self-reflection and meeting the demands of the organization—a skill that Heifetz calls "adaptive leadership."[47] Carving out time

---

44  Ronald Heifetz, Alexander Grashow and Martin Linsky, *The Practice of Adaptive Leadership: Tools and Tactics for Changing Your Organization and the World* (Boston, MA: Harvard Business Press, 2009), 6.

45  Heifetz et al., *Adaptive Leadership*, 7.

46  Ronald Heifetz and Marty Linsky, "A Survival Guide for Leaders," *Harvard Business Review* 80 no. 6 (June 2002): 65-74, 152.

47  Heifetz et al., *Adaptive Leadership,14.*

to think and reflect have helped me to keep pace with the changing dynamics of today's technology-fueled work environment. As Warren Bennis said, "The manager has his eye on the bottom line; the leader has his eye on the horizon."[48]

## KEY TAKEAWAYS

The foundations of great leadership start with owning your personal identity, an integral part of your emotional intelligence. I think of emotional intelligence as the secret sauce of effective leadership. Each of us possesses a unique combination of ingredients that are a product of our personal history. Identity is the lens through which we view the world—our history, our culture, and our beliefs. No two leaders have the exact same mix of ingredients, so each of us has a unique perspective that impacts how we think and feel about any given situation. Our uniqueness is the real beauty that comes from leading with our identities. Bringing your secret sauce, your identity, and your whole self into the workplace adds a unique flavor that enhances the whole environment.

For me, owning my identity has been one of the most important steps in developing emotional intelligence. I've had to embrace who I am and where I came from in order to gain control of my emotions. The more I've grown to understand and accept myself, the easier it is to put myself in others' shoes. As the Greek philosopher Socrates said, "To know thyself is the beginning of wisdom."[49]

---

48   Will Yakowicz, "Lessons from Leadership Guru Warren Bennis," Inc., August 4, 2014, accessed June 10, 2020.

49   Meg Selig, "25 Fun and Helpful Quotations About the Human Mind," *Changepower* (blog), *Psychology Today*, November 17, 2016.

# CHAPTER 3

# YOUR BRAIN ON LEADERSHIP

—

We are what we think. All that we are arises with our thoughts. With our thoughts, we make the world.

—BUDDHA[50]

I have a confession to make, I'm a chronic procrastinator. I'm the queen of the eleventh-hour deliverable. I could never understand why I put off finishing projects until the last possible second. If a report is due at 5:00 p.m., I'm the person hitting send at 4:59 p.m., praying the computer cooperates. My lifelong procrastination habit is stressful, but at the same time, impending deadlines move me to action.

---

50  Meg Selig, "25 Fun and Helpful Quotations About the Human Mind," *Changepower* (blog), *Psychology Today*, November 17, 2016.

During my leadership coaching certification training at Georgetown University's Institute for Transformational Leadership, I gained insights into neuroscience—the study of the anatomy and physiology of the brain—and its impact on my behaviors. The brain is the seat of connection, strategy, and self-awareness. A basic of understanding of neuroscience is essential for leaders to understand themselves and others around them.

Our brains play a major role in our identity—how we see the world, how others perceive us, and how we interact with others. Understanding the role the brain plays in leading others is one of the most important tools in a leader's toolkit. Like any good tool, knowing how to use it safely and effectively is vital.

## YOUR THREE-POUND CONTROL CENTER

The human brain controls all of your bodily functions and interprets and processes information from the outside world. Rick Hanson, author of *Buddha's Brain: The Practical Neuroscience of Happiness, Love & Wisdom*, wrote, "Your brain is 3 pounds of tofu-like tissue containing 1.1 trillion cells, including 100 billion neurons. On average each neuron receives about five thousand connections, called synapses." Comprising roughly 2 percent of our body's weight, the brain uses about 20 percent of our oxygen and glucose. The brain works as a system receiving information from the five senses: hearing, sight, smell, taste, and touch.[51] Understanding how your brain works is important to gaining mastery of how we impact the world. Let's start with an overview of the brain and its impact on emotions, connection, and leadership.

In the 1960s, neuroscientist Paul D. MacLean introduced the idea of the triune brain. His model divides the brain into three regions:

The base of the brain closest to the spinal cord is the basal ganglia, sometimes referred to as the primitive or reptilian brain.

The limbic system sits roughly in the middle of your brain and is sometimes referred to as the emotional brain.

The neocortex is located at the front of your brain behind the forehead and is sometimes referred to as the executive suite.[52]

The reptilian or primitive area of the brain is responsible for the most basic survival functions, such as heart rate, breathing, body temperature, and spatial orientation. The key function of the limbic system is to react to external factors by initiating the fight-or-flight response to danger. The limbic system consists of the hippocampus,

---

51  Rick Hanson and Richard Mendius, *Buddha's Brain: The Practical Neuroscience of Happiness Love & Wisdom* (Oakland, CA: New Harbinger Publications, 2009).

52  John Newman and James Harris, "The Scientific Contributions of Paul D. MacLean (1913–2007)," *The Journal of Nervous and Mental Disease* 197 (2009): 3-5.

the amygdala, and the hypothalamus. The hippocampus encodes events and moves them from short-term to long-term memory, the amygdala makes extremely fast but not always accurate evaluations of potential threats, and the hypothalamus initiates a response to stress by pumping out hormones.[53]

Finally, the neocortex houses the prefrontal cortex or "executive suite," which is responsible for functions such as concentration, organization, judgement, reasoning, decision-making, creativity, emotional regulation, social-relational abilities, and abstract thinking. The prefrontal cortex responds to stimuli in a relatively slow and deliberate manner and can be "hijacked" by the faster limbic system or the even faster reptilian brain.[54]

MacLean suggests that the brain evolved over the millennia, starting with its control over the most primitive autonomic functions such as breathing and moving housed in the basal ganglia. Next, as the limbic system developed, the brain became able to produce emotions and store memories. Finally, with the development of the neocortex, the brain can complete higher cognitive functions such as complex thinking. MacLean's triune brain theory oversimplifies the complexity of how the human brain works, but it does provide an easily digestible model.[55]

---

53  "Anatomy of the Brain," Mayfield Clinic. Accessed June 23, 2020.

54  Adele Diamond, "Executive Functions," *Annual Review of Psychology* 64 (2013): 135-68.

55  Andreas Komnios, "The Concept of the 'Triune Brain," Interaction Design Foundation, accessed June 23, 2020.

## THE BRAIN IS YOUR EMOTIONAL AND
## SOCIAL SENSE ORGAN

Emily Esfahani Smith, author of *The Power of Meaning: Crafting a Life That Matters*, said, "Given the size of our bodies, our brains should be much smaller—but they are by far the largest in the animal kingdom relative to our body size. The question is why." Smith continued, "Scientists have debated this question for a long time, but the research of anthropologist Robin Dunbar is fairly conclusive on this point. Dunbar has found that the strongest predictor of a species' brain size—specifically, the size of its neocortex, the outermost layer—is the size of its social group. We have big brains in order to socialize."[56]

University of California, Los Angeles (UCLA) social neuroscience researcher Naomi Eisenberg found that the feeling of being excluded provokes the same sort of reaction in the brain that physical pain might cause. After examining someone who had been excluded, she said, "We saw activity in the neural region involved in the distressing component of pain, or what is sometimes referred to as the 'suffering' component of pain."[57] Another UCLA neuroscience researcher, Matthew Lieberman, hypothesized that the link between social connection and physical discomfort within the brain exists "because, to a mammal, being socially connected to caregivers is necessary for survival." This study and many others now emerging have made one thing clear: the human

56  Emily Esfahani Smith, "Social Connection Makes a Better Brain," The Atlantic, October 29, 2013.

57  Naomi Eisenberger, Matthew Lieberman, and Kipling Williams, "Does Rejection Hurt? An fMRI Study of Social Exclusion," *Science* 302 no.5643 (November 2003): 290-292.

brain's physiological and neurological reactions are directly and profoundly shaped by social interaction. As Lieberman said, "Most processes operating in the background when your brain is at rest are involved in thinking about other people and yourself."[58]

After learning about this research, finding out that one of the most important leadership skills is the ability to relate and connect to others comes as no surprise. Scott Edinger, frequent contributor to the *Harvard Business Review*, writes, "The ability to make an emotional connection is so often misunderstood because it's not about being emotional or showing emotion. It's about making a human connection—one person to another."[59] He also argues that since leaders accomplish their work through other people, the focus should be on the quality of the leader's connections as much as the outputs or products of the team.

## THE NEUROSCIENCE OF LEADERSHIP

In this chapter so far, we've learned that neuroscience is the study of how the nervous system and the brain works. Now, let's take a look at the brain from the perspective of a leader. Dr. David Rock coined the term "neuroleadership" to refer to the application of neuroscience to leadership development, management training, change management, and coaching.[60]

---

58  *TED*, "Matthew Lieberman: The Social Brain and Its Superpowers," October 7, 2013, video, 6:23.

59  Scott Edinger, "Three Ways Leaders Make Emotional Connections," *Harvard Business Review*, October 12, 2012.

60  David Rock, "The Neuroscience of Leadership," Your Brain at Work (blog), *Psychology Today*, March 10, 2011.

Tobias Kiefer, former director of global learning and development at Booz & Company, describes neuroleadership as "the art of synchronizing the science of the brain with leadership behaviors." He believes leaders should learn to "go limbic—move out of the cerebral, intellectual zone and be challenged at a physical and emotional level." Kiefer thinks that if emerging leaders learn about neuroleadership, they'll be able to understand the impact that emotions and behaviors have on their successes and failures.[61]

Dr. Rock believes leaders need to have a language to describe mental experiences. He said, "One of the first ideas from brain research to make its way into leadership is the idea of an amygdala hijack—suddenly there is language for telling others that your brain is shutting down."[62] The following section will give you a sense of what an amygdala hijack looks like and how it can affect you at work.

## FIGHT OR FLIGHT

Unlike the cavemen, most of the threats we face today are psychological. However, our brains don't always differentiate between a physical threat and a threat to our self-esteem. The primitive part of our brain evolved to deal with physical threats to our survival that required a quick response. As a result, our body still responds with fight or flight even though there's no actual physical threat with which we must contend.

61  Tobias Kiefer, "Neuroleadership – Making Change Happen," *Leadership* (blog), *Ivey Business Journal*, May/June 2011.

62  David Rock, *Your Brain at Work: Strategies for Overcoming Distraction, Regaining Focus, and Working Smarter All Day Long* (New York: Harper Business, 2020).

The amygdala also activates the limbic system, where all of our old memories are stored. Once triggered, this part of the brain begins to remember other similar threats and lumps them together. New threats combined with remembered offenses serve to exacerbate the reaction, frequently blowing the actual issue out of proportion.

Dr. Bessel van der Kolk called the amygdala the brain's "smoke detector" in his book *The Body Keeps the Score: Mind, Brain, and Body in the Healing of Trauma*. When we perceive a threat, the amygdala sounds an alarm, releasing a cascade of chemicals in the body. A rush of stress hormones floods the body within 0.07 seconds, much faster than the prefrontal lobe, which regulates the executive function in 0.1 seconds. The three signs of the amygdala hijack are a strong emotional reaction, the sudden onset of that reaction, and then regret for your actions once you have a chance to reflect on the incident.[63]

Dr. Matthew Lieberman found an inverse relationship between the amygdala and the prefrontal cortex, which houses the brain's executive function, rational thought, and judgment. When we experience psychological stress such as an amygdala hijack, our amygdala becomes active with blood and oxygen and there's less activation in our prefrontal cortex.[64] Since the blood and oxygen are in the amygdala instead of the prefrontal cortex, we experience disrupted thinking and have trouble problem solving—it's like losing

---

63  Bessel Van der Kolk, *The Body Keeps the Score: Brain, Mind, and Body in the Healing of Trauma* (New York: Viking, 2014).
64  Eisenberger, Lieberman, and Williams, "Does Rejection Hurt?", 290-292.

ten to fifteen IQ points temporarily. Fortunately, this loss of IQ points is temporary.[65]

One way to gain back your lost IQ points after an amygdala hijack is to label your feelings so you can normalize what you're experiencing. Putting a label on your feelings and thinking of the emotions as a data set of information helps us to accept, manage, and adjust to those emotions. Emotions are just as important as our thoughts, if not more, given their power to overwhelm us.

You can prevent or stop an amygdala hijack by breathing, slowing down, and trying to focus your thoughts. This allows your frontal cortex to regain control so that you can choose the most reasonable and appropriate way to respond to the situation. Psychology blogger Arlin Cuncic said, "One can prevent an amygdala hijack's consequences by using the 6-second rule. Waiting for just six seconds causes the brain chemicals that cause amygdala hijacking to diffuse away. Just take a deep breath and try to look at something pleasant or imagine a pleasant memory. It prevents your amygdala from taking control and causing an emotional reaction. This gets better with time."[66]

## THE MELTDOWN

The atmosphere in the crowded conference room three hours into what should have been a thirty-minute briefing was

---

65  Relly Nadler, "Where Did My IQ Points Go," *Leading with Emotional Intelligence* (blog), *Psychology Today*, April 29, 2011.
66  Arlin Cuncic, "Amygdala Hijack and the Fight or Flight Response," *Emotions* (blog), *Verywell Mind*, June 16, 2020.

tense. Half of the room played on their smart phones while the other half tried not to make eye contact. Out of nowhere, one of the team leads made a snarky comment, wondering aloud, "Whose stupid idea was this anyway?" In the space of a few seconds, Allison, the project manager, turned bright red. Her hands shook and a stream of expletives poured out of her mouth as she stormed out of the room.

We had just witnessed a normally cool, level-headed person "lose it" in front of her team. Allison's "meltdown" triggered a flashback to a time in my own career when I had an uncharacteristic outburst because I felt disrespected by a peer. I can't remember what he said, but I let a string of profanity fly out of my mouth before my better judgment kicked in. That event left me feeling shaken, embarrassed, and full of regret. Looking back, my reaction was totally out of proportion to the perceived slight. I wondered what triggered this type of behavior and how could I stop it from happening again.

These potentially career-ending outbursts that Allison and I both experienced were the result of an amygdala hijack—a personal, emotional response that's immediate, overwhelming, and out of proportion with the perceived threat.

Psychologist Daniel Goleman first used the term "amygdala hijack" in his 1995 book, *Emotional Intelligence: Why It Can Matter More Than IQ.* Goleman credits renowned neuroscientist, researcher, and author Joseph E. LeDoux with laying the foundation for our understanding of the amygdala.[67]

---

67  Daniel Goleman, "The Battle of the Brain," On Talent and Leadership, *Briefings Magazine*, accessed August 25, 2020.

LeDoux found that "the architecture of the brain gives the amygdala a privileged position as the emotional sentinel, able to hijack the brain."[68]

The world witnessed one of the most bizarre amygdala hijacks ever recorded on a sweltering Las Vegas night in the summer of 1997. "Iron" Mike Tyson and Evander "The Real Deal" Holyfield met in the boxing ring for the World Boxing Association (WBA) Heavyweight Championship. During the fight, Holyfield headbutted Tyson, creating a gash over his eye. In an apparent rage, Tyson bit Holyfield's left ear, removing a chuck of ear cartilage. As a result of his behavior, Tyson lost the fight by disqualification, the Nevada State Athletic Commission revoked his boxing license, and he had to pay a $3 million fine. Tyson later regretted his action and in a 2009 appearance on the Oprah Winfrey Show, he apologized to Holyfield. The apology paved the way for the two men to develop a close friendship.[69] According to Daniel Goleman, "When Mike Tyson bit Evander Holyfield's ear, it was a very bad business decision—it cost him $3 million. It was an amygdala hijack."[70]

Whether your experience with an amygdala hijack happens in front of a crowded conference room, in a boxing ring, or with a loved one, understanding why they happen and what you can do to prevent them in the future is important.

---

68  Joseph LeDoux, "The Amygdala," *Current Biology* 17, no.20 (2007): R868-74.

69  *The Oprah Winfrey Show*, "Remembering Mike Tyson's Apology to Evander Holyfield," June 27, 2016.

70  Nadler, "Where Did My IQ Points Go."

## THREATS TO IDENTITY

Amygdala hijacks can also occur when your identity is threatened. Research conducted over a four-year period by University of Virginia Professor Peter Belmi found that social identity threats can be even more powerful than personal threats. Dr. Belmi's research also demonstrated that the desire for respect is universal. "There are substantial costs when people feel that they are not accorded the respect that they think they deserve."[71] Disrespect, slights, and subtle bias are harmful both in one's personal life and in the workplace. When people feel devalued because of their identity, their performance and creativity suffer.

According to Daniel Goleman, the opposite of an amygdala hijack is emotional intelligence. He argues that emotional intelligence is "the ability to perceive emotions, to access and generate emotions so as to assist thought, to understand emotions and emotional knowledge, and to reflectively regulate emotions so as to promote emotional and intellectual growth."[72] The emotionally intelligent person is engaged, focused, motivated, and attentive, and can determine which of these skills to use during the situation at hand.

If, like me, you do find yourself in the aftermath of a full-blown amygdala hijack, take some time to acknowledge your actions and review what happened. The aftermath of my personal amygdala hijack taught me a valuable lesson in

---

71  Peter Belmi et al, "Threats to Social Identity Can Trigger Social Deviance," *Personality and Social Psychology Bulletin* 41, no. 4 (April 2015): 467–84.

72  Daniel Goleman, *Emotional Intelligence: Why It Can Matter More Than IQ* (New York: Bantam Books, 1995).

humility. I knew the only way to repair the damage done by my outburst was to take a critical look at myself. I realized my reaction had more to do with things that had happened in the past than with the minor incivility of my peer. I had to take ownership of my inappropriate behavior and apologize to my colleague. Being willing to admit I had been wrong allowed us to rebuild trust. While our brains are hardwired to protect us against threats—both real and perceived—increasing emotional intelligence can help us take charge of both our actions and reactions.

## CHANGING HABITS: NEURONS THAT FIRE TOGETHER WIRE TOGETHER

The best leaders are always learning new habits and behaviors to develop their skills. Our habits and behaviors create neural pathways, comprised of neurons connected by dendrites, in our brain. The number of dendrites increases along with the frequency with which we perform a behavior, kind of like how grooves form in well-traveled roads. Our brain cells communicate with each other via a process called "neuronal firing." Psychologist Deann Ware explains that when brain cells communicate frequently, the connection between them strengthens and "the messages that travel the same pathway in the brain over and over begin to transmit faster and faster." With enough repetition, these behaviors become automatic.[73]

Reading, driving, and riding a bike are examples of complicated behaviors we do automatically because neural pathways

---

73 Deann Ware, "Neurons that Fire Together Wire Together–But Why? Hebb's Rule and Synaptic Plasticity," *Awareness* (blog), accessed June 23, 2020.

have formed in our brains. Scientists have estimated that it takes ten thousand repetitions to master a skill and develop the associated neural pathway and three to six months for a new behavior to become a habit. According to registered nurse Julie Hani, the best way to form new neural pathways is to use all five senses; "Connecting a new behavior to as many areas of the brain as possible helps to develop new neural pathways."[74]

Researchers are discovering the potential for behavior change through a process called neuroplasticity—the ability of the brain to form new connections and pathways and change how its circuits are wired. When we learn, we form new pathways in the brain. Through repetition and over time, these pathways become wired in our brains to form habits—automatic behaviors we do somewhat unconsciously. The basal ganglia or reptilian brain is crucial for habit forming.[75]

In his groundbreaking book *Hardwiring Happiness: The New Brain Science of Contentment, Calm, and Confidence,* neuropsychologist Dr. Rick Hanson explains that our brains are wired toward the negative. He argues that if we have ten experiences during the day—five neutral everyday experiences, four positive experiences, and one negative experience—we're probably going to think about that one negative experience before going to bed that night. Fortunately, *Hardwiring Happiness* provides a strategy for interrupting this tendency: by focusing on the good for ten to twenty seconds,

---

74  Julie Hani, "The Neuroscience of Behavior Change," *Improving Health Outcomes* (blog), Cecelia Health Marketing, April 18, 2019.

75  Susannah Cahalan, *Brain On Fire: My Month of Madness* (New York: Simon & Schuster, 2012).

you give the brain time to absorb and store the experience in long-term memory.[76]

Dr. Tim Pychyl, head of the Procrastination Research Group (yes, there really is such a thing!), found that procrastination is a struggle between these two systems in the brain—the amygdala and the limbic system. He describes procrastination as "a dance between the amygdala or the limbic system, the emotional brain, and the prefrontal cortex." The good news is, Dr. Pychyl reported, "Eight weeks of mindfulness meditation actually shrink the size of the amygdala."[77] Changing the neural connections to the prefrontal cortex can actually break the procrastination cycle. So, there's hope for me and other chronic procrastinators!

## KEY TAKEAWAYS

Every brain is different because of the distinctive history that informs our identity. We all have own unique experiences that have shaped our brain and continue to shape it throughout our lives. Neuroscience and neuroleadership have helped me understand why I procrastinate and how I can change my behavior and build new habits.

Roman philosopher Marcus Aurelius aptly summed up the importance of understanding how your brain works. "You

---

76  Rick Hanson, *Hardwiring Happiness: The New Brain Science of Contentment, Calm, and Confidence* (Westminster, MD: Random House, 2013).

77  Fushia Sirois, Timothy Pychyl, "Procrastination and the Priority of Short-Term Mood Regulation: Consequences for Future Self, *Social and Personality Psychology Compass* 7 no. 2): 115–127.

have power over your mind—not outside events. Realize this, and you will find strength."[78] Learning to understand yourself, your behaviors, and your habits is a critical component of emotional intelligence.

Emotions and connection are the keys to great leadership. Developing control over those emotions and avoiding amygdala hijacks are necessary for fostering lasting connections. As leaders, we have the ability to change our brains by practicing new behaviors that can lead to new habits. Repetition plays an important role in changing these behaviors.

The practice of mindfulness emphasizes attention and focus, making your brain more capable of overruling the limbic system and getting more done due to an improved attention span. I'm still working on sustaining my mindfulness practices, but I can attest that they're helping me reduce my tendency to procrastinate.

---

78  Marcus Aurelius and Gregory Hays, *Meditations* (New York: Modern Library, 2002).

## CHAPTER 4

# THE CHEMICAL COCKTAIL OF TRUST AND BELONGING

---

To wake the giant inside ourselves, we have to be faithful to our own eccentric nature, and bring it into conversation with the world.

–DAVID WHYTE[79]

The brain actually determines trustworthiness within milliseconds of meeting a person.[80] As a result, fostering employees' trust and giving them a sense of belonging are

---

79  David Whyte, *Crossing the Unknown Sea* (New York: Penguin Group, 2002), 51.

80  Janine Willis and Alexander Todorov, "First Impressions: Making Up Your Mind After a 100-MS Exposure to a Face," *Psychological Science* 17 no. 7 (2006): 592-8.

fundamental to fostering healthy organizations. Such organizations can accomplish this with great leaders.

The primary focus of a good leader is to build positive relationships with their teams.[81] Noted psychologist and researcher Richard Boyatzis describes effective leaders as those individuals who are able to build trusting, engaged, and energizing relationships with others around them.[82]

## YOUR BRAIN ON TRUST

A 2008 study discovered that when someone's brain releases a chemical called oxytocin, that person is more receptive to feeling trust toward a stranger.[83] Neuroeconomist Paul Zak found that if you treat someone well, their brain produces oxytocin, which makes them motivated to treat you well, too. Applied to the workplace, the oxytocin released by all employees treating their colleagues with respect creates a culture of trust. According to Zak, "Employees in high-trust organizations are more productive, have more energy at work, collaborate better with their colleagues, and stay with their employers longer than people working at low-trust companies."[84] The chemical cocktail of oxytocin seems to lead to better performance.

---

81 Ibid.

82 Richard Boyatzis and Annie McKee, *Resonant Leadership: Renewing Yourself and Connecting with Others Through Mindfulness, Hope, and Compassion* (Boston: Harvard Business School Press, 2005).

83 Paul Zak, "Why Inspiring Stories Make Us React: The Neuroscience of Narrative," *Cerebrum: The Dana Forum on Brain Science* 2015, no. 2 (February 2015).

84 Paul Zak, "The Neuroscience of High-Trust Organizations," *Consulting Psychology Journal: Practice and Research* 70, no. 1 (2018): 45–58.

People in high-trust organizations tend to suffer less chronic stress and are generally happier with their lives. Pricewaterhouse Coopers (PwC) reported in its 2016 global survey that 55 percent of CEOs think a lack of trust is a threat to the organization's growth. PwC also found that people at high-trust companies report 74 percent less stress, 106 percent more energy at work, 50 percent higher productivity, 13 percent fewer sick days, 76 percent more engagement, 29 percent more satisfaction with their lives, and 40 percent less burnout compared to people at low-trust companies.[85]

## BELONGING = HAPPINESS

Research conducted by the Center for Talent Innovation reports that employees who have a sense of belonging are three and a half times more likely to contribute to their fullest potential.[86] The emotional impacts of belonging and exclusion are such important issues in the workplace that consulting firm Ernst & Young (EY) launched a study called the EY Belonging Barometer.[87]

The study surveyed one thousand employed US adults spanning different generations, genders, and ethnicities. Researchers found that more than 40 percent of those surveyed felt physically and emotionally isolated in the workplace. On a positive note, the study also found that 39 percent reported

---

85  Paul Zak, "The Neuroscience of Trust," *Harvard Business Review* (January – February 2017): 84 – 90.

86  "Power of Belonging: What It Is and Why It Matters in Today's Workplace," Center for Talent Innovation, accessed July 2, 2020.

87  Karyn Twaronite, "Five Findings on the Importance of Belonging," EY, accessed July 2, 2020.

feeling the greatest sense of belonging when their colleagues checked in with them both personally and professionally. This simple act can clearly make a tremendous difference in helping employees feel like they belong.[88]

The EY Belonging Barometer substantiated findings from research conducted by the global health services company Cigna and UCLA. This survey used the UCLA Loneliness Scale to gauge loneliness, on which a score of forty-three or higher indicates loneliness. The Cigna study surveyed more than twenty thousand US adults aged eighteen years and older found that nearly half of Americans report sometimes or always feeling alone (46 percent) or left out (47 percent).[89]

## THE POWER OF BELONGING

A line ran done the walkways and around the block in front of the majestic Washington National Cathedral on a clear, cold January day in 2018. I was one of hundreds of people gazing up at the stately neo-gothic spires of the cathedral, waiting to hear a sermon from best-selling author and University of Houston professor Dr. Brené Brown. The irony of Dr. Brown—who can be equal parts profound and profane—preaching a sermon to a crowd in Washington, DC, added to the anticipation. Dr. Brown has made the study of courage, vulnerability, shame, and empathy her life's work, and I couldn't wait to hear her speak.

---

88  Karyn Twaronite, "The Surprising Power of Simply Asking Coworkers How They're Doing," *Harvard Business Review* (February 2019).

89  "2018 Cigna Loneliness Index," Cigna, accessed July 2, 2020.

As I walked into the cathedral and took my seat, I was struck by a sense of history that permeated through this place. These walls had seen state funerals for three US presidents and memorials services for five other presidents. Rev. Dr. Martin Luther King Jr. preached his final Sunday sermon from the Cathedral's Canterbury Pulpit just days before his assassination in the spring of 1968.

The priests interrupted my thoughts as they walked in with their ceremonial purple, white, and gold robes. Bringing up the rear of the procession was the head of the Episcopal church in his bishop's robes and Brené Brown in a simple sweater, corduroy pants, and short boots. The contrast in appearance between the clergy and Dr. Brown was rather jarring. To her credit, she held her head high and walked in with the confidence of someone who's comfortable in their own skin.

Dr. Brown stepped up to the pulpit and started the sermon with the traditional Episcopalian greeting, "Peace be with you," the first and last traditional aspect of the service. She discussed her faith journey and referred to her relationship with God as "an amazing love story." She told us about her early years in Catholic school and her struggles with alcohol in college. She referred to her struggles as a "briar patch. . . not enough sleep, too much work, too many expectations, resentment, perfecting, pleasing, proving, and a few other thorny things." She realized that "what had been dressed up as hard living was really addiction and mental health issues." In 1996, two weeks before she was scheduled to graduate from college, she had a pivotal call with her mother. After that call, she stopped drinking and smoking and went to her first Alcoholics Anonymous meeting.

## BELONGING MEANS BEING WHO YOU ARE

In her sermon, Dr. Brown discussed our need to belong and to be a part of a community. The idea of belonging appears as a theme in much of her writing and lectures. In her book *Braving the Wilderness: The Quest for True Belonging and the Courage to Stand Alone*, she writes that belonging is an innate need we all have to be a part of something bigger than ourselves.[90]

In *The Gifts of Imperfections: Let Go of Who You Think You're Supposed to Be and Embrace Who You Are*, she writes that fitting in and belonging are not the same thing. She believes that fitting in can actually get in the way of belonging. Fitting in is all about being who you think you need to be in order to gain acceptance. By contrast, "Belonging doesn't require us to change who we are, it requires us to be who we are."[91] I say a big amen to that!

Brené Brown opened her heart to each of us in that cathedral. Her authenticity and vulnerability give her the uncanny ability to make everyone in her presence feel like the most important person in the room. At the end of the service, Bishop Mariann Edgar Budde, the first woman to be elected bishop and leader of the forty-five thousand Episcopalians in Washington, DC, articulated what we all felt: "You embody your own belonging and you give each of us permission to do the same."

---

90  Brené Brown, *Braving the Wilderness: The Quest for True Belonging and the Courage to Stand Alone* (New York: Random House, 2017), 31.

91  Brené Brown, *The Gifts of Imperfection: Let Go of Who You Think You're Supposed to Be and Embrace Who You Are* (Center City, MN: Hazelden Publishing, 2010), 25.

## WORDS CREATE WORLDS

Words have power. This old saying has been around forever, but I never knew why until I met Judith E. Glaser. Judith was a best-selling author, researcher, and top executive coach. The first words she said to me packed the punch of a heavyweight fighter: "Words create worlds." This statement would have made sense coming from a fiction writer or poets, not from a world-renowned organizational anthropologist and executive coach.

I met Judith E. Glaser on a brutally cold winter morning in 2018 at the quarterly breakfast meeting of the DC Neuroleadership Group. This group, the brainchild of its founder, author and executive coach Wendy Swire, is a word-of-mouth, members only "salon" that has been meeting in downtown Bethesda, Maryland, for over ten years. It reminds me of an underground supper club for neuroscience geeks.

The quarterly meetings draw a diverse mix of business leaders, executive coaches, mental health professionals, academics, government leaders, and consultants. It's an engaging community that has attracted prominent guest presenters including researchers, scientists, authors, professors, psychologists, and other recognized experts in fields pertaining to applied neuroscience. Despite our differences, each member comes hungry to learn more about the tangible and practical applications of cutting-edge brain science.

## THOUGHTS ARE INTERNAL WORDS

Judith started her talk by asking the group if they remembered where they were on September 11, 2001. Of course, every hand in the room went up. She said, "On 9/11, I was in my doctor's office in Manhattan waiting for a fax that would tell me if I had cancer. As I watched the smoke from the Twin Towers, I got the news that I had Stage 4 breast cancer. It was the first of many diagnoses. The cancer has spread to my lungs and I'm now fighting pancreatic cancer." Judith told us that her mother had seven bouts with cancer before she passed away. She was twenty-two years old when her mother died, which made her question how long she would live.

Everyone in the room sat in stunned silence. How could she be so calm and composed? Judith explained that over the last seven years, she had to take charge of her treatments. She had a double mastectomy that never healed after her second bout with cancer. She tried to tell her doctors that something was wrong, but they ignored her. They later discovered that she had underlying, inoperable Stage 4 pancreatic cancer. She said, "I fired my first oncologist because his negativity was getting in the way of my healing." Then, Judith found doctors who knew the power of words. She said, "I refused to allow negativity to enter my mind." Her doctors could only speak words of hope, encouragement, and healing.

Judith continued, "Thoughts are internal words that create internal and external worlds." She began to research the impacts of words and conversations while fighting cancer. During her long battles with cancer, she wrote her seminal book, *Conversational Intelligence: How Great Leaders Build Trust and Get Extraordinary Results.* She told us, "Conversational intelligence gives us the power to influence our neurochemistry, even in the moment. It turns out that human beings are hardwired to have conversations impact them in such profound and significant ways that it can actually turn genes on and off."[92]

Judith's brilliance showed itself at an early age. She became interested in human behavior at a young age, reading medical books by eleven years old and entering college at sixteen. She earned her bachelor's degree from Temple University and later attended Drexel University. where she received a research fellowship and a master's degree in human behavior and development, which included related work at Harvard University's Bales School of Social Relations. She also earned a master's certificate in corporate and political communications from Fairfield University. Judith was certified to administer twenty assessments used for individuals, teams, and organizations, and she created four assessments based on her Conversational Intelligence methodology. In 2006, she received the Gallery of Success Award from Temple University.

Judith was a founding member of the Harvard Institute of Coaching, a partnership of executive coaches and organizational consultants. She served as an adjunct professor at the University of Pennsylvania's Wharton School of Business and a visiting guest speaker at schools including Harvard, Northwestern University's Kellogg School of Management, Loyola, and the University of Chicago. Her clients included companies such as Clairol, Donna Karan, Pepsi, Citibank, IBM, AT&T, and Pfizer. She authored seven books and was the senior editor of the Random House Handbook of Business Terms.

---

92 Judith E. Glaser, *Conversational Intelligence: How Great Leaders Build Trust and Get Extraordinary Results* (Brookline, MA: Bibliomotion, Inc, 2014), xx.

## CONVERSATIONAL INTELLIGENCE

Judith E. Glaser was a phenomenal woman. Her curiosity and passion for sharing knowledge drove her to create the Conversational Intelligence for Coaches (C-IQ) program in 2016. Over thirty-two thousand professionals attended the initial program over the course of three years. Eight hundred and thirty professional coaches from around the world, including myself, completed the C-IQ Certification.[93]

Judith's health began to fail in the summer of 2018, but she was determined to remain an active part of the C-IQ program. She tirelessly recorded video lessons for the time when she could no longer teach the program. She wanted her legacy to carry on.

Judith passed away on November 18, 2018.

I'll always remember her favorite saying: "To get to the next level of greatness depends on the quality of the culture, which depends on the quality of relationships, which depends on the quality of conversations. Everything happens through conversations."[94]

## KEY TAKEAWAYS

One of the prime responsibilities of effective leadership is creating an environment in which others can flourish. Without a culture that promotes trust and helps make everyone feel they belong, an organization suffers.

---

93  "C-IQ Certification," The CreatingWE® Institute, accessed July 3, 2020.
94  Glaser, *Conversational Intelligence.*

Great leaders open pathways of trust in their employees' brains. Those pathways lead to employee engagement and a positive work environment. The chemical oxytocin sets the stage for trust, released when others treat us well. In turn, the oxytocin released makes that person want to treat others well. Even something as simple as saying, "Good morning. How are you doing today?" is all it takes to give someone a healthy dose of oxytocin and begin the cycle of trust and belonging. Leaders can leverage oxytocin's domino effect to radically change the climate of an organization.

Belonging is a primal human need. Leaders who cultivate a culture of trust and belonging reap a harvest of goodwill. Little things like checking in on a colleague adds up to a greater sense of belonging.  As Judith E. Glaser wrote, "Mastering our moments of contact is the art of great leadership."[95]

Finally, remember that a leader's words can create worlds. Everything happens through conversations and relationships. What kind of a worlds are your words creating?

---

95  Ibid.

# PART TWO

# THE INTERSECTION OF LEADERSHIP AND IDENTITY

# CHAPTER 5

# EMBRACING YOUR IMPERFECTIONS

———

When we were children, we used to think that
when we were grown-up we would no longer be
vulnerable. But to grow up is to accept vulnerability. To be alive is to be vulnerable.

–MADELEINE L'ENGLE[96]

Humans have an ingrained desire to be seen and understood,
but you can't truly be seen and understood until you let down
your guard. Vulnerability takes courage. In my early years
as a leader, walking into meetings and not seeing a single
person who looked like me sent the signal that vulnerability
was not an option.

---

96  Madeleine L'Engle, *Walking On Water: Reflections on Faith & Art*
    (Wheaton, IL: H. Shaw, 1980).

I spent so many years struggling under the weight of expectations. As a leader, a woman, and a person of color, I always felt like I needed to be perfect. The need for perfection grew out of my own insecurities, feelings of unworthiness, and bearing the burden of being the "only." Many times, I was the "only" woman of color in leadership, so I felt like I was always under the microscope being judged.

## THE LEADERSHIP CONNECTION

Gallup found that 65 percent of employees are "not engaged" or "actively disengaged" at work.[97] As a result, they're "less emotionally connected" and also "less likely to be productive." However, honest, authentic connections can bring people together in the workplace. Psychology professor Paula Niedenthal's research showed that "we are programmed to observe each other's states so we can more appropriately interact, empathize, or assert our boundaries, whatever the situation may require."[98] Creating connections through vulnerability can have a domino effect through the workplace and greatly improve morale.

Dr. Niedenthal defines "resonance" as an automatic process that allows humans to read each other's expressions in a very nuanced way. Resonance often occurs below our level of conscious awareness. Her finding shows that we resonate at such a deep subconscious level with one another that

---

97 Jim Harter, "Historic Drop in Employee Engagement Follows Record Rise," Gallup, July 2, 2020, accessed September 3, 2020.

98 Emma Seppälä, "What Bosses Gain by Being Vulnerable," *Harvard Business Review* (December 11, 2014).

inauthenticity cannot be ignored.[99] Authentic leaders own their stories, identities, and flaws.

Having a harsh inner critic can be an obstacle when trying to connect with others. Clinical psychologist Lisa Firestone describes the inner critic as "those nagging thoughts that tell us we are not good enough, that cast doubt on our goals and undermine our accomplishments." Everyone has an inner critic that provides a negative commentary on our actions, appearance, and behaviors.[100]

When I first began my leadership journey, my inner voice amplified my feelings of unworthiness, making it hard for me to be vulnerable and make connections with others. I tried to hide feelings of unworthiness by putting up a mask to keep others from seeing the real me.

## TRANCE OF UNWORTHINESS

Tara Brach is a Buddhist meditation teacher who blends Western psychology and Eastern spiritual practices. Her unique background unites the logic of neuroscience with the heart-centered practices of mindfulness. The result is a distinctive voice of Western Buddhism that offers a wise and caring approach to freeing ourselves and society from suffering.[101]

99  Lisa Firestone, "4 Ways to Overcome Your Inner Critic," *Compassion Matters* (blog), *Psychology Today*, May 14, 2013.

100  Tori DeAngelis, "A blend of Buddhism and Psychology," *Monitor on Psychology,* February 2014.

101  Tara Brach, "Allow Life to Be Just As It Is: Interview with Clementine Van Wijngaarden," accessed September 3, 2020.

Tara graduated with a double major in psychology and political science from Clark University. During college, she began attending yoga classes and exploring Eastern approaches to inner transformation. On a weekend camping trip with an older and wiser friend, Tara came to a realization: "Something is fundamentally wrong with me." Her wise friend told her she needed to learn to be her own best friend. This idea shook Tara to her core because she didn't trust or like herself enough to be her own best friend. Reflecting back, Tara understands that she was caught in the "trance of unworthiness" at the time. She describes this "trance" as the gap between who we should be and our moment-to-moment experiences. It's the feeling of not being okay, of being harassed by an interior judge. Her struggle to fix her brokenness had manifested itself into an addiction to food and a preoccupation with achievement.[102]

In her early twenties, Tara embarked on the path to enlightenment. She became a self-described type A yogi, driven to reach enlightenment. She was so focused on racing toward Nirvana that she missed the true goal of Buddhism: self-acceptance. As she continued to learn more about the teachings of Buddha, she gradually learned to view her life with compassion. She also let go of the mistaken notion that she was alone in her suffering.[103]

Tara eventually lived in an ashram—a spiritual community—where she practiced and taught both yoga and concentrative meditation for ten years. When she left the ashram and

---

102 Ibid.

103 *Sounds True*, "Waking Up from the Trance of Unworthiness with Tara Brach," May 22, 2019, video, 31:33.

attended her first Buddhist Insight Meditation retreat, she realized she was home. "I had found wisdom, teachings, and practices that train the heart and mind in unconditional and loving presence," she explained. "I knew that this was a path of true freedom."[104]

Even after twenty years of meditation practice, Tara can still get caught in the "trance of unworthiness." Over the last decade, Tara has had bouts with a debilitating illness. At her lowest moments, she can be irritable and self-centered, which makes her fall into the "trance" of not liking herself for being the negative sick person and for not being spiritual enough. In those moments, she feels like she's hit by what the Buddha calls the second arrow. The first arrow is the "I'm sick." The second arrow is "I'm unworthy."[105]

## RADICAL ACCEPTANCE

Tara believes that feelings of unworthiness are one of the most pervasive problems humans face. Feeling unworthy leads to loneliness and isolation. As humans, we're predisposed to a negative bias and know something could always go wrong, but we also have the capacity to "tend and befriend" others as well as ourselves.[106]

Waking up from the "trance of unworthiness" has been the focus of much of Tara's work over the last fifteen years. She

---

104 Ibid.

105 *Tara Brach,* "Attend and Befriend: Healing the Fear Body," May 28, 2012, 1:00.26.

106 Tara Brach, *Radical Acceptance: Embracing Your Life with the Heart of a Buddha* (New York: Bantam Books, 2004).

believes in the possibility of emotional healing and spiritual awakening through mindful, loving awareness as well as the alleviation of suffering in the world by practicing compassion in action.[107]

Tara's four-step practice for radical acceptance that unites mindfulness and compassion helps to shift us from the "trance" state to self-acceptance. Her practice is called RAIN, which stands for Recognize, Allow, Investigate, and Nurture. Recognize your thoughts and feelings, allow them to exist, investigate with kindness what is happening in your body, and nurture the spirit of wholeness.[108]

Tara is a shining example of one of her favorite phrases: "You don't have to live a limiting story of yourself." Despite her illness, she's providing a path for the rest of us to free ourselves from the "trance of unworthiness," silence the inner critic, and open the door to courageous vulnerability.[109]

## LETTING GO OF THE SHELL

In the summer of 2017, I found myself at a crossroad. I was contemplating a significant career change: moving from the security of a successful thirty-year career in the federal government to the uncertainty of starting my own business. I had just completed the Georgetown University Institute for Transformational Leadership's coaching certification program. Georgetown's motto, cura personalis—care of the

---

107 Ibid.
108 *Sounds True,* "Trance of Unworthiness."
109 Lisa Firestone, "Inner Critic."

whole person—inspired me to take an honest look at who I was as a leader and as a human being. Months of self-reflection turned into a journey to find my true self, not just the image I projected to the world.

I've spent most of my life living in a protective shell. Self-doubt, stress, longing, and loneliness hid behind my mask of poise and success; my calm exterior hid my inner pain. I would peek out occasionally to sample life, but when I felt overwhelmed or insecure, I retreated back to the safety of my shell. While my shell gave me protective armor, it limited my ability to feel, to love, to hurt, and to grow.

I began to recognize that the image I projected was incongruent with the master assessment that dominated my inner world: I'm not good enough. Inwardly, I kept thinking, "If everyone knew the real me, they wouldn't like me."

So, during that long, hot summer of 2017, I began to imagine a different possibility. What if I took a chance on living free from my armor, free from fear? What if I could silence my inner critic?

Clinical psychologist and researcher Lisa Firestone suggests that the most effective way to quiet your inner critic is by identifying what it's trying to tell you, separating the voice from the reality of who you are, and acting against the destructive thought process.[110]

---

110  Peter Economy, "17 Wise Nelson Mandela Quotes That Will Inspire Your Success," accessed July 3, 2020.

I spent a lot of time trying to change my narrative through affirmations and self-talk in order to build myself up on the inside to match the outside. I identified that my inner critic's voice was telling me I wasn't good enough, so I replaced that old narrative with the truth: "I am enough."

My imperfections, my struggles, and my story are what contribute to my greatness. I had to stop beating myself up for not being perfect and for thinking I had to pretend to be someone other than who I am in order for people to accept me. Letting go of unrealistic expectations and learning to silence my inner critic helped me to appreciate my strengths.

## KEY TAKEAWAYS

Nelson Mandela once said, "There is no passion to be found playing small—in settling for a life that is less than the one you are capable of living."[109] Great leaders play big. They're risk-takers. They open themselves up to failure, ridicule, and rejection every day and know the secret of leadership is courage. You need courage to be vulnerable and to show up with your whole heart.

Great leaders know that in order to build a successful team, they must set a compelling vision, connect with each team member, and help the team connect with each other. There's no connection without vulnerability.

I decided to write *Dropping the Mask* to pull back the curtain on the struggles of women in leadership and the disconnect between our public identities and the way we think of ourselves internally. I know that constantly holding up the mask is exhausting. It's my mission to help leaders reclaim their true identities by reconciling their inner and outer personas. Helping others gain the confidence to lead with their whole hearts gives me the strength to truly be my best self and gives me the courage to own my story.

## CHAPTER 6

# INCLUSIVE LEADERSHIP

---

Fear is so fundamental to the human condition
that all the great spiritual traditions originate in
an effort to overcome its effects on our lives. With
different words, they all proclaim the same core
message: "Be not afraid." Though the traditions
vary widely in the ways they propose to take us
beyond fear, all hold out the same hope: we can
escape fear's paralysis and enter a state of grace
where encounters with otherness will not threaten
us but will enrich our work and our lives.

−PARKER J. PALMER[111]

---

111  Parker Palmer, *The Courage to Teach: Exploring the Inner Landscape of a Teacher's Life* (San Francisco, CA: Jossey-Bass, 1998).

Women of color will make up the majority of all women by 2060, meaning they'll become the majority of the US workforce.[112] With the changing face of leadership on the horizon, understanding what it means to lead through our personal lens of identity and culture becomes increasingly important.


## BEGINNINGS OF OTHERNESS

As a little brown girl growing up in Jacksonville, Florida, in the 1960s, my world revolved around my family and a community of people who looked like me. I went to segregated schools, lived in an all-Black middle-class neighborhood, and went to Sunday School with others who shared a similar background. Most of us were teachers' kids.

My first sense of otherness happened when I was in second or third grade. At that time, schools were separate but certainly not equal. On the first day of school, our teacher told us that we had gotten "new" books. I vividly remember opening the cover of a battered old book to read the stamp on the inside of the front cover: "Discarded by Lake Forest Elementary School."

Minority schools like mine rarely received new books and supplies. We got the leftovers and the castoffs from white schools like Lake Forest. On that first day of school, the teacher took what seemed like hours trying to find enough usable books for everyone in the class. We flipped through the ragged books, many with missing pages or graffiti

---

112  Catalyst, *Quick Take: Women of Color in the United States* (March 19, 2020).

scrawled in the margins. The feeling of unworthiness seeped into my spirit as we dug through the stacks of books. I kept thinking we weren't good enough to have new books. What other reason could there be for giving us books that should've gone in the garbage? I think that was my first real moment of recognizing that the world viewed me as something different because of my skin color.

That feeling of otherness remains in me to this day. Even now, I can't stand used books. All the way through college and graduate school, I never wanted to use someone else's books. I couldn't even bring myself to use a highlighter until graduate school. There's something sacred about a clean, crisp book with all the pages intact. I love the sound of ruffling through the pages of a pristine book.

## DIVERSITY, INCLUSION, AND BIAS

Bias, otherness, and prejudice in society and in the workplace have a significant impact on women and people of color. Throughout my career, I frequently found myself as the only woman, the only African American, or the only African American woman, which can be lonely and demotivating. Former First Lady Michelle Obama describes this feeling: "My experiences have made me far more aware of my 'Blackness' than ever before. I have found that no matter how liberal and open-minded some [people] try to be toward me, I sometimes feel like a visitor, as if I really don't belong."[113]

---

113 Jeffrey Ressner, "Michelle Obama Thesis Was on Racial Divide," Politico, February 23, 2008, accessed September 4, 2020.

Jennifer Eberhardt has been interested in issues of race and bias since she was a child. That fascination with understanding bias led her to earn a PhD from Harvard University in psychology. She received a 2014 MacArthur Foundation "Genius Grant" Fellowship and is one of the world's leading experts on unconscious racial bias.

Dr. Eberhardt grew up in an all-Black neighborhood in Cleveland, Ohio. Her parents wanted a better education for their children, so they decided to move to the predominantly white Cleveland suburb of Beachwood. In a recent NPR interview, Dr. Eberhardt recalled that shortly after moving to Beachwood, she noticed something strange: she could no longer tell people's faces apart. She could still recognize the faces of her family, but she couldn't distinguish the white faces of her new neighbors and classmates.[114]

As an adult, Dr. Eberhardt coined a name for this phenomenon: the "cross-race effect" or "other-race effect." This effect speaks to the tendency for people across all races to be better at recognizing faces of their own race than those of other races. For children, this phenomenon may just be confusing, but Dr. Eberhardt has found that it could lead to harmful, racist behavior in adults.[114]

In 2019, Dr. Eberhardt released *Biased: Uncovering the Hidden Prejudice That Shapes What We See, Think, and Do.* In this book, she explains how all of us are vulnerable to racial

---

114 "Jennifer Eberhardt: Can We Overcome Racial Bias? 'Biased' Author Says to Start by Acknowledging It," interview by Ailsa Chang, March 28, 2019, NPR, podcast, 7:48.

bias.[115] She says, "The 'cross-race effect' is like a precursor for bias, basically, because if your brain isn't processing those faces, you're not able to individuate the faces." Since the brain likes to subconsciously categorize everything, "once you put a face in a category then that can also trigger your beliefs and feelings about the people who are in that category."[116] This type of labeling can also cause us to treat other types of people differently.

Dr. Eberhardt said during an interview with CBS *This Morning*, "I think typically when people think about bias, they're thinking about burning crosses and people filled with hate." She added that bias affects everyone—you don't have to be a bigot or a bad person to have bias. She also explained that the situations in which we find ourselves can trigger our biases, and some situations make us more vulnerable to acting on bias than others.[117]

## WIRED FOR BIAS

Dr. Eberhardt believes the foundations of bias are wired into our brains from infancy. She's reported that babies as young as three months already show a preference for faces of their own race. She says, "This starts early. I mean, it has to do with who we're surrounded by, and our brains get conditioned to looking at those faces and being able to distinguish among them."[118]

---

115  Jennifer Eberhardt, *Biased: Uncovering the Hidden Prejudice That Shapes What We See, Think, and Do.* 2019.

116  Ibid.

117  CBS This Morning, "You don't have to be a bigot to have bias," March 25, 2019, video, 6:26.

118  Eberhardt, *Biased.*

Research in the past decade has found that bias, both explicit and implicit, may be more of a function of the brain rather than deliberate choice. As human beings, we innately perceive anyone different from ourselves as a threat because our brain has an evolutionary requirement to do so. "The capacity to discern 'us' from 'them' is fundamental in the human brain," wrote David Amodio, associate professor of psychology and neuroscience at New York University.[119] He explained, "Although this computation takes just a fraction of a second, it sets the stage for social categorization, stereotypes, prejudices, intergroup conflict and inequality."[120]

As we learned in Chapter 3, the amygdala is the part of the brain that receives direct input from all sensory organs, enabling it to respond rapidly to immediate threats before higher level cognitive functions can respond. It also triggers the fight-or-flight response and reacts to social threats in the same way as physical threats.[121] Additionally, the amygdala greatly affects how we interact in social situations.

Social scientist Walter Lippmann was the first to apply the idea of stereotyping to the social sciences. He argued that it would be too exhausting for our brains to constantly see everything individually and in detail rather than as types

---

119  Chris Bergonzi, "Understanding Bias and the Brain," Korn Ferry Institute, accessed July 6, 2020.

120  Ibid.

121  Ibid.

and generalities; human brains are just not equipped to deal with so much subtlety.[122]

Dr. Eberhardt supports this theory. She says that our cognitive systems continuously sort perceived elements into categories and subcategories so that we can function effectively in the world. We use our prior experience with and cultural knowledge of categories to form expectations about what will happen next. Those expectations influence our behavior. If our brains didn't apply categorical knowledge before we've had a chance to consciously reflect, we'd experience everything as if for the first time.[123]

As such, Dr. Eberhardt says implicit bias can enter our lives in many areas, even for people who don't believe they're racist or bigoted. Leaders must understand that bias can creep into our evaluation of others, how we assign choice assignments, and the factors we use to decide on promotions and whom we hire. At the end of the day, bias isn't an affliction we can cure or banish. Dr. Eberhardt reminds us, "It's a human condition that we have to understand and deal with."[124]

## THE ECONOMIC IMPACT OF DIVERSITY

By every measure, companies with the most ethnically diverse executive teams were 33 percent more likely to outperform their peers on profitability, and those with

---

122  Walter Lippmann, *Public Opinion,* (New York: Harcourt, Brace and Company, 1922), 102-103.

123  Eberhardt, *Biased.*

124  Ibid.

executive-level gender diversity worldwide had a 21 percent likelihood of outperforming their industry competitors.[125] A recent study of venture capital firms found that more diverse teams had higher financial returns than their homogenous counterparts.[126]

Despite the economic benefits of diversity, companies haven't been great at promoting women of color to senior roles. The *Women in the Workplace 2019* report on gender equality found that Black women are even more likely to aspire to hold a powerful position with a prestigious title than white women.[127] Yet Black women's advancement into leadership roles has remained stagnant, even as their numbers in professional and managerial roles has increased.[128]

## BROKEN RUNGS ON THE CORPORATE LADDER

We often talk about the glass ceiling that prevents women from reaching senior leadership positions. In reality, the biggest obstacle women face occurs much earlier in the pipeline at the first step up to manager. I believe fixing this broken rung is key to achieving parity.

The glass ceiling is a term introduced more than forty years ago to define invisible, systemic barriers that prevent women from rising to senior leadership. Lean In and McKinsey & Company's 2019 annual report on the state of

---

125  Vivian Hunt et al, *Delivering Diversity* (McKinsey & Company, 2018).

126  Ibid.

127  Jess Huang et al, *Women in the Workplace 2019* (LeanIn, McKinsey & Company, October 2019).

128  Ibid.

women in the workforce found that the glass ceiling isn't the biggest obstacle to women's progression; instead, the greatest obstacle for women and people of color ascending to the C-suite is the first step of the leadership ladder: the broken rung.[129]

For every one hundred men promoted and hired to manager, only seventy-two women are similarly promoted and hired. This discrepancy results in more women than men getting stuck in entry-level positions and fewer women becoming managers. In addition, men end up holding 62 percent of manager-level positions while women hold just 38 percent, which has a long-term impact on the talent pipeline. This means there are significantly fewer women to choose from than there are men for hiring or promoting to senior management positions.

Furthermore, the numbers of women decrease at every subsequent level up the ladder. Even with the current progress in hiring and promotion rates for women at senior levels, they will never be able to catch up because of the scarcity of women at the first step on the management ladder available to advance to the highest levels. Black women and Latinas are even more likely to be derailed by the broken rung than white women. For every one hundred entry-level men promoted to manager, just sixty-eight Latinas and fifty-eight Black women are promoted. In addition, for every one hundred men hired to manager, fifty-seven Latinas and sixty-four Black women are hired.[130]

---

129 Ibid.
130 Ibid.

More than half of HR leaders and employees think their company will reach gender parity in leadership over the next ten years. In reality, it'll take many decades for us to reach gender parity at the highest ranks. The compelling case for fixing the broken rung is powerful. If women are promoted and hired to first-level manager at the same rate as men are, an additional one million more women will need to be added to management positions in corporate America over the next five years.[131]

## 'ONLY' THE LONELY

Women are underrepresented throughout the corporate pipeline and many end up being the only or one of the only women in the room. The *Women in the Workplace 2019* report found that one in five women says they're often an "Only," and this experience is twice as likely for senior-level women and women in technical roles. By comparison, only 5 percent of men are the only or one of the only men in the room, and—regardless of their race, ethnicity, or sexual orientation—they face less scrutiny than women Onlys.

The work experience for women Onlys can be difficult. The report indicated that Onlys are far more likely to experience microaggressions than women who work with other women. Onlys are more than twice as likely to be asked to prove their competence, over three times more likely to be mistaken for someone more junior, and roughly twice as likely to be subjected to demeaning or disrespectful remarks.[132]

---

131  Ibid.
132  Ibid.

## EMOTIONAL TAX

An emotional tax is the associated detrimental effects from the experience of being different from peers because of gender, race, or ethnicity. Asian, Black, Latinx, and multiracial professionals in the United States experience an emotional tax as they aspire to advance in and contribute to their organizations.[133] Black employees experience a heightened awareness of their difference in the workplace, which manifests itself in disruptive sleep patterns, reduction of their sense of "psychological safety," and diminishing of their ability to contribute fully at work. Despite this feeling of exclusion, 88 percent of black women reported wanting to remain in the same organization, 87 percent still want to be an influential leader, and 81 percent are working toward a high-ranking position.[134]

## KEY TAKEAWAYS

Understanding how bias and stereotyping works in the brain has helped me recognize my own biases, which allows me to make better decisions. As Dr. Eberhardt said, "We open our minds to the personal growth that comes with diversity. And each day provides us with a new opportunity to practice being our best selves."[135]

---

133   Georges Desvaux et al, *Women Matter 2017* (McKinsey & Company, 2017).

134   Dnika J. Travis, Jennifer Thorpe-Moscon, and Courtney McCluney, *Emotional Tax: How Black Women and Men Pay More at Work and How Leaders Can Take Action* (Catalyst, 2016).

135   Eberhardt, *Biased.*

The economic and moral imperative for increasing the women, people of color, and other underrepresented groups in the workplace is clear. Rebekah Steele, senior fellow in Human Capital and program director at the Conference Board summed this up beautifully: "By better understanding the lived experiences of different individuals and diverse groups of employees, we are better able to create systems and process that support the meaningful engagement of a broad mix of talent and to tap into the unique value proposition of each diverse person."[136]

The growing demand for justice and equality should offer hope for those of us with diverse identities to thrive in the workplace.

---

136 Ibid.

# CHAPTER 7

# THE CHANGING FACE OF LEADERSHIP

——

Change will not come if we wait for some other person or if we wait for some other time. We are the ones we've been waiting for. We are the change that we seek.

–PRESIDENT BARACK OBAMA[137]

In the next thirty years, current minorities will become the majority in the United States; Hispanic, Black, Asian, and other racial minorities will make up a majority of the population by 2050.[138] The changing demographics of the United States will have a significant impact on the face of the US

---

137  "Barack Obama's Feb. 5 Speech," *New York Times*, February 5, 2008.
138  U.S. Census Bureau, "Projected Race and Hispanic Origin: Main Projections Series for the United States, 2017-2060," U.S. Census Bureau, Population Division: Washington, DC, accessed July 11, 2020.

workforce and on its leadership. To understand where we're headed, it helps to understand the current landscape and the role identity plays in leadership.

Our identity defines who we are, and who we are is how we lead. Our identities are based on a complex mix of characteristics such as race, gender, sexuality, class, religion, and nationality. The changing demographics in the workplace requires us all to embrace people with different identities. University of Washington Professor Anu Taranath wrote, "I think we can develop empathetic feelings and sort of crack open our sense of self to include other people's experiences in it."[139]

The traditional models of leadership and leadership development are no longer relevant. The future of leadership requires us to throw out the cookie-cutter models and adapt to leading with and through identity. Moving forward, leaders will also need to have a firm grasp of diversity, equity, and inclusion in order to engage and connect with the changing face of the US workforce. If leaders are able to do this, I believe the shifting demographic has the potential to profoundly and positively disrupt the work environment.

## IDENTITY IS RESILIENCE

My concept of who I am and the identities I hold evolves over time. There are aspects of identity that I was born with, such as genetics, race, and sex. There are other aspects that

---

139  Ruth Terry, "Travel is Said to Increase Cultural Understanding - Does it?", National Geographic, July 13, 2020.

are impacted by my environment, like family dynamics, geographic location, and life experiences. My identity is as unique as my fingerprint. No one on this Earth is exactly like me. As I'm learning and growing as a human, my identity is changing, too.

I can't count the number of times I've walked into a room and been the only one who looks like me. Whether I'm conducting a meeting, presenting, or giving a speech, my identity as a woman of color is usually the first thing people see. I'm carrying an extra burden my white colleagues will never have to face. In those times when I'm feeling overwhelmed from being the Only, I hear a voice in my head telling me, "Get it together, get up, keep moving. We're here." My inner cheerleaders are reminding me, "We've gone through a whole lot worse. It's time for you to shake it off and get back in the game."

One of the traps I fell into early in my career was thinking I needed to measure myself against external standards, but the majority culture always sets the standards and picks the measuring stick. If I could go back to the past, I would tell my twenty-five-year-old self to stop defining herself by someone else's standards. My older, wiser self has learned that painful lesson, and now I know the truth: when I define myself based on other people's expectations, I'll always come up short. The standard of white masculinity imposes itself onto minorities, so we often measure ourselves against an ideal we'll never be able to achieve. When we define ourselves based on somebody else's perceptions or standards, we're devaluing our own unique identities. I'm never going to be a white male, nor do I want to be.

I don't wake up in the morning and think, "I'm a Black woman"; I just wake up in the morning feeling good about being me. I've learned to love who I am and to use my own internal measuring stick to make sure I reach my goal of being the best person I can be. I ask myself each day, "How can I make myself better for humanity?"—not just to be better than Suzy or Jim for the next promotion. One of the traps I fell into early in my career was thinking I needed to measure myself against external standards.

I so appreciate the sacrifices my forebearers endured in order for me to even be able to get into the room or onto the stage. I often think about whose shoulders I'm standing.

## IDENTITY IS FLUID

Over the past decade, more people have begun to acknowledge that their identities don't fit in with the existing conceptions of gender, race, and ethnicity. In many areas of the world, society is moving forward to reflect this change, but business has not. Recent research on demographic identities in organizations found that 95 percent of prior studies used demographic identities based on traditional ideas of gender, race, and ethnicity. The most troubling finding indicated that employees who identify in ways that do not conform to traditional categories are more likely to feel marginalized and even threatened at work.[140]

---

140 Beth Humberd, Judy Clair and Elizabeth Rouse, "Employee Demographics Don't Have to Be at Odds with Employees' Identities," *Harvard Business Review* (January 24, 2020).

Before we dive any deeper, we must start with a few definitions. Keep in mind, these definitions aren't the same things
as labels. I have a word of caution about labels: everyone's
identity is built on how we see ourselves and the personal
descriptors that we embrace. Generalizations and stereotypes can cloud perceptions and lead to misunderstandings.
My advice is when in doubt, ask the person how they identify themselves and what descriptors they are comfortable
with using.

## Race and Ethnicity

Sociologists Michael Omi and Howard Winant developed
the racial formation theory that views race as a socially con-
structed identity. As such, social, economic, and political
forces determine the content and importance of racial categories. They argue that "race is an unstable and 'de-centered'
complex of social meanings constantly being transformed by
political struggle."[141]

Classifications of race and ethnicity have evolved since the
first US decennial census in 1790 to the latest count in 2020.
Categorical names have changed over the years to reflect
current politics, science, and public attitudes. For example,
the US Census Bureau eliminated the use of "colored" and
replaced it with "black," later adding "Negro" and "African
American." For the 2020 decennial census, the term "Black
or African American" is used. Census workers determined
the race of the people they counted up until the 1950 census.

---

141  Michael Omi and Howard Winant, *Racial Formation in the United
States,* (New York: Routledge, 2015).

Beginning in 1960, Americans could choose their own race. In 2000, Americans could include themselves in more than one racial category, allowing multiracial people this option for the first time.[142]

## THE CHANGING DEMOGRAPHICS OF THE WORKPLACE

In today's environment, there are few women and people of color in the ranks of senior leadership. A *New York Times* article noted, "In the corridors of American power, it can be as easy to find a man named John as it is to find a woman."[143] However, a sea change is happening that will open new avenues for women in leadership. It stands to reason that women of color will be at the forefront of the changing face of leadership.

The Pew Research Center predicts that the US population will change significantly by the year 2050. Non-Hispanic whites currently make up 67 percent of the population will decline to 47 percent by 2050. The Hispanic population will increase from 14 percent of the population today to 29 percent in 2050. The Black population in the US will not change from the current 13 percent level by 2050. Asians, who currently make up 5 percent of the population, will increase to 9 percent in 2050.[144]

---

142 Anna Brown, "The Changing Categories the U.S. Census Has Used to Measure Race," Pew Research Center, February 25, 2020, accessed July 11, 2020.

143 Claire Miller, Kevin Quealy, and Margot Sanger-Katz, "The Top Jobs Where Women Are Outnumbered by Men Named John," *The New York Times*, April 24, 2018.

144 Kim Parker, Rich Morin and Juliana Horowitz, "America in 2050," Pew Research Center, March 21, 2019, accessed July 11, 2020.

Slightly more than half of all babies born in the United States today are a racial or ethnic minority, a threshold first crossed in 2015. These minorities currently make up about 40 percent of the overall population, but they're projected to increase to 56 percent by 2060, according to US Census Bureau projections.[145]

Demographer William Frey's research reveals that people of color will fuel the population growth for the next several decades. He explained, "Minorities will be the source of all of the growth in the nation's youth and working age population, most of the growth in its voters, and much of the growth in its consumers and tax base as far into the future as we can see."[146]

The American Sociological Association (ASA) is a national organization established over a century ago in order to advance the scientific discipline of sociology. The ASA's twenty thousand sociologists have come to the consensus that "race" refers to physical differences that groups and cultures consider socially significant, while "ethnicity" refers to shared culture such as language, ancestry, practices, and beliefs.[147]

The US Census Bureau also defines race and ethnicity as two separate and distinct concepts. Race is "a person's

---

145 Jens Manuel Krogstad, "A View of the Nation's Future Through Kindergarten Demographics," Pew Research Center, July 21, 2019, accessed July 11, 2020.

146 William Frey, *Diversity Explosion: How New Racial Demographics Are Remaking America* (Washington, D.C: Brookings Institution Press, 2018).

147 "Race and Ethnicity," American Sociological Association, accessed July 18, 2020.

self-identification with one or more social groups." Those social groups are White, Black or African American, Asian, American Indian and Alaska Native, Native Hawaiian and other Pacific Islander, or another race. Individuals have the option to identify and report multiple races. In contrast, according to the Census Bureau, ethnicity determines "whether a person is of Hispanic origin or not." They divide ethnicity into two categories: "Hispanic or Latino" and "Not Hispanic or Latino." Hispanics have the option to report as any race.[148]

Sociology professors Stephen Cornell and Douglas Hartmann define race as "a human group defined by itself or others as distinct by virtue of perceived common physical characteristics that are held to be inherent....Determining which characteristics constitute the race. . . is a choice human beings make. Neither markers nor categories are predetermined by any biological factors."[149] Cornell and Hartmann define ethnicity as a sense of common ancestry based on cultural attachments, past linguistic heritage, religious affiliations, claimed kinship, or various physical traits.

Society at large is now frequently using the acronym BIPOC to describe people of color. BIPOC, which stands for Black, Indigenous, and People Of Color, is pronounced "buy-pock." According to the BIPOC Project, use of the term "aims to build authentic and lasting solidarity among Black, Indigenous and People of Color (BIPOC), in order to undo Native

---

148  U.S. Census Bureau, "About Race," accessed July 11, 2020.
149  Stephen Cornell and Douglas Hartmann, *Ethnicity and Race: Making Identities in a Changing World* (Thousand Oaks, Calif: Pine Forge Press, 2007).

invisibility, anti-Blackness, dismantle white supremacy and advance racial justice."[150]

In addition to race and ethnicity, culture is a uniting factor for a group of people. Anthropologist Cristina De Rossi believes culture "encompasses religion, food, what we wear, how we wear it, our language, marriage, music, what we believe is right or wrong, how we sit at the table, how we greet visitors, how we behave with loved ones, and a million other things."[151] She also argues that culture is fluid and ever changing. "Culture appears to have become key in our interconnected world, which is made up of so many ethnically diverse societies, but also riddled by conflicts associated with religion, ethnicity, ethical beliefs, and, essentially, the elements which make up culture."[152]

## GENDER IDENTITY

The Human Rights Campaign (HRC) is the largest national lesbian, gay, bisexual, transgender and queer (LGBTQ) civil rights organization with over three million members.[153] The HRC defines gender identity as "one's innermost concept of self as male, female, a blend of both or neither—how individuals perceive themselves and what they call themselves. One's gender identity can be the same or different from their sex assigned at birth." The HRC's *Talking About Pronouns in the*

---

150 Kendra Cherry, "What Does the Acronym BIPOC Mean?", Race and Identity (blog), *Very Well Mind*, June 24, 2020.

151 Kim Ann Zimmermann, "What Is Culture. Live Science, July 13, 2017, accessed July 11, 2020.

152 Ibid.

153 Human Rights Campaign (@HRC), "HRC is the nation's largest LGBTQ civil rights organization," Twitter, October 28, 2020, 3:40 pm.

*Workplace* guide advises, "Since some pronouns are gendered ('she/her' and 'he/him') it is important to be intentional about the way we use pronouns as we all work to create as inclusive an environment as possible."[154]

Gender identity is not always visible since it's determined by an individual's sense of how they see themselves. Also, gender identity is not fixed—it can be fluid. In today's environment, a growing number of employees are entering the workplace with gender identities and expressions that may be different from traditional categorization. The HRC suggests, "While many transgender people identify on a binary scale— as either male or female—some do not and may instead refer to themselves as 'genderqueer,' 'gender fluid,' 'non-binary' or other terms." Many people who do not identify with one of the two traditional binary genders use pronouns such as 'they/them.' Using a person's chosen name and desired pronouns is a form of mutual respect and a basic courtesy.[155]

Our society's acceptance of individual identity is slowly but surely evolving to become more inclusive, and concepts such as race, ethnicity, and gender identity are becoming more fluid. Our identities are complex and growing less binary over time.

Beth Ford made history in 2018 as the first openly gay woman to lead a major US Fortune 500 company when she became CEO of Land O'Lakes, the century-old agricultural cooperative based in Minneapolis, Minnesota. She also became the

---

154   "Pronouns 101," Human Rights Campaign, accessed July 11, 2020.
155   "Talking About Pronouns in the Workplace," Human Rights Campaign, accessed July 11, 2020.

third openly gay person to serve as the CEO of a Fortune 500 company, following Apple's Tim Cook and the Dow Chemical Company's James Fitterling.

Land O'Lakes has yearly revenues of over $15 billion, employs over ten thousand people, and is the largest producer of butter and cheese in the United States. Ford told CNN, "I made a decision long ago to live an authentic life. If my being named CEO helps others do the same, that's a wonderful moment." She later stated in an interview with *Fortune Magazine*, "I think it must be really hard if you feel like you're in a culture where you can't be who you are. Work is hard enough, and then when you have to feel as though you can't be who are, that's got to be incredibly difficult."[156]

Ford's CEO appointment provided a beacon of hope for the LGBTQ community; unfortunately, one month before the historic announcement, the HRC published a survey that found 46 percent of all US workers who identify as LGBTQ say they're closeted at work.[157] Deena Fidas, director of workplace equality at the HRC, welcomed Ford's appointment, telling CNN, "This is not a story of someone getting into the higher echelons of leadership and then coming out. This is someone walking into this role with her full self." Fidas also hailed the selection on the HRC website, saying, "Her authentic leadership as an out lesbian is well-known in the

---

156 Curtis Wong, "New Land O'Lakes CEO Is First Openly Gay Woman To Head A Fortune 500 Company," *Huffington Post*, July 30, 2018, accessed July 11, 2020.

157 Elliott Kozuch, "Startling Data Reveals Half of LGBTQ Employees in the U.S. Remain Closeted at Work," Human Rights Campaign, accessed July 11, 2020.

LGBT corporate community, and the fact that she is assuming this role as an out lesbian sends an especially powerful message."[158]

Despite this great achievement for the LGBTQ community, many businesses still use outdated organizational categorization systems to organize people into demographic groups. Judith A. Clair, Beth K. Humberd, Elizabeth D. Rouse, and Elise B. Jones conducted research to better understand current assumptions about gender, race, and ethnicity at work. They found that past practices and outdated governmental regulations require many businesses to classify an employee's race, gender, and ethnicity using traditional, binary terms.[159]

Traditional categorizations can have an adverse impact on employees and customers who don't see their identities reflected in limiting labels. The researchers found that "employees who identify in ways that do not conform to the norms used to define and categorize them at work are more likely to feel marginalized, and even threatened." They went on to conclude that these employees' "motivation, engagement, performance, and overall satisfaction at work can suffer."[160]

## MILLENNIALS AND GEN Z-ERS

Who qualifies as a "millennial" or "Gen Z-er" can vary depending upon the source used to gather the data. The US

---

158  Wong, "Land O'Lakes CEO."
159  Judith A. Clair et al, "Loosening Categorical Thinking: Extending the Terrain of Theory and Research on Demographic Identities in Organizations," *Academy of Management* 44 (2019): 592–617.
160  Humberd, Clair and Rouse, "Employee Demographics."

Census Bureau previously defined a millennial as a someone born between 1982 and 2000, but they've also stated that "there is no official start and end date for when millennials were born."[161] The Pew Research Center considers anyone born between 1981 and 1996 to be a millennial, and anyone born 1997 and later to belong to Gen Z.[162] A 2019 Pew report found that a greater acceptance of the "fluidity and multiplicity of identity" exists among millennials and Gen Z-ers more than with prior generations. The report found 35 percent of Gen Z-ers and 25 percent of millennials know someone who uses gender-neutral pronouns. Nearly 60 percent of Gen Z-ers and 50 percent of millennials believe pronouns other than "he" and "she" should be included as options on forms and profiles that ask for gender information.[163]

Deloitte, one of the world's largest consulting firms, conducted a study in 2018 of more than ten thousand millennials (born 1983–1994) and 1,800 people from Gen Z (born 1995–1999). They posed questions about how these generations define diversity. Deloitte found that only 17 percent of millennials and 24 percent of Gen Z respondents mentioned aspects of demographics, lifestyle, or faith; the respondents believed diversity includes tolerance, inclusiveness, openness, respect, and acknowledgment of different ideas or ways of thinking. The study also found that respondents who think

---

161  U.S. Census Bureau, "The Changing Economics and Demographics of Young Adulthood: 1975–2016," accessed July 11, 2020.

162  Michael Dimock, "Defining Generations: Where Millennials End and Generation Z Begins," Pew Research Center, January 17, 2019, accessed July 11, 2020.

163  Kim Parker and Ruth Igielnik, "On the Cusp of Adulthood and Facing an Uncertain Future: What We Know About Gen Z So Far," Pew Research Center, May 14, 2020, accessed July 11, 2020.

diverse organizations with diverse senior leaders are more attuned to ethics, more creative, more effective at talent development, and more effective at nurturing emotional intelligence.[164]

Furthermore, the study found that "69 percent of employees who believe their senior management teams are diverse see their working environments as motivating and stimulating (versus 43 percent of younger workers who don't perceive their leadership teams as diverse)." They also observed a correlation between diversity and successful business outcomes: 78 percent of millennials who say their top teams are diverse report that their organizations perform strongly in generating profits, a number 13 percentage points higher than that of leadership teams that aren't diverse.[165]

## KEY TAKEAWAYS

As Mahatma Gandhi said, "A nation's culture resides in the hearts and in the soul of its people."[166] Identity, culture, and gender are fluid like a meandering river. Our identities evolve over time as we develop over the course of our lives.

Today's cultural values, beliefs, and societal norms are changing with increased diversity and the emergence of the next generations of leaders. Binary forms of gender identification no longer work in today's complex work environment. Being open to individual definitions of identity and the stories each

---

164  "The Deloitte Millennial Survey 2018," Deloitte, accessed July 11, 2020.
165  Ibid.
166  MK Gandhi Foundation, "Civilization and Culture," accessed July 11, 2020.

individual brings to work is essential to nurturing a healthy work environment.

For young leaders of color, the mission is to answer the question, "Who is it that you want to be?" I believe you should be who were you put on this Earth to be, not be who society tells you to be. You'll need to discover your true identity in order to do so and emerge on the other side of the game of leadership sane and whole. Fortunately, the changing demographics of the workforce opens the door for a greater appreciation for each person's unique identity.

The path ahead is about defining yourself. The key is to create your own measuring stick.

# CHAPTER 8

# THE UNEVEN PLAYING FIELD

———

No matter how big a nation is, it is no stronger
than its weakest people, and as long as you keep
a person down, some part of you has to be down
there to hold him down, so it means you cannot
soar as you might otherwise.

−MARIAN ANDERSON[167]

Imagine getting dressed in your best power suit and designer
pumps for a media event you arranged for a candidate for
the US Senate. When you and the candidate arrive at the
venue, you tell the receptionist, "We're here for the lunch."
The receptionist motions for you to follow her and she

---

167  Brian Kurian, "Shining A Light on Racism," Medium, April, 20, 2019,
      accessed October 4, 2020.

unceremoniously ushers you to the kitchen. She looks at you and says, "Where are your uniforms?"[168]

The receptionist assumed that the two people standing in front of her were there to serve lunch. It never occurred to her that one of these women was Mellody Hobson, the president and co-CEO of Ariel Investments and the former chairwoman of DreamWorks Animation SKG, which annually rakes in over $15 billion in box office sales. Hobson also negotiated NBCUniversal's $3.8 billion acquisition of DreamWorks Animation. Additionally, she sits on the board of directors of companies like JPMorgan Chase and the Sundance Institute, and she's vice chair of Starbucks. In 2017, she became the first African American woman to head the Economic Club of Chicago.[169]

Mellody Hobson told this story during a 2014 TED Talk that now has almost 4 million views.[170] She continued her story, saying that to make matters worse, the man accompanying her was Harold Ford Jr., a successful businessman, former Congressman, and candidate for the US Senate. Hobson asked the audience rhetorically, "Now, don't you think we need more than one Black person in the US Senate?" In a recent interview with CBS This Morning, she said, "My race is one of the first things that people see" and that some people never look beyond her skin color. Despite all of Hobson's accomplishments, she's still not

168 *TED*, "Color Blind or Color Brave?" May 5, 2014, video, 14:14.
169 Bethany McLean, "Why Sheryl Sandberg, Bill Bradley, and Oprah Love Mellody Hobson," *Vanity Fair Magazine*, March 30, 2015.
170 *TED*, "Color Brave."

immune to the discrimination perpetrated against women of color every day.[171]

## TWENTY-FIRST-CENTURY RACISM

Racism today can be subtle, covert, and indirect, which makes it hard to define and sometimes even more difficult to deal with. Even identifying racism can sometimes be difficult because it can be expressed through microaggressions rather than traditional, overt racism.[172] Although it may be covert, the damage of racism can be deep and long-lasting.

Aversive racism is a form of contemporary racism that, in contrast to the traditional form, operates unconsciously in subtle and indirect ways. Aversive racists regard themselves as nonprejudiced while subconsciously harboring negative feelings and beliefs about members of minority groups. Sociologists originally used the concept of aversive racism to characterize the attitudes that many well-educated white liberals in the United States had toward the Black community. The basic principles of aversive racism apply to the attitudes of members of dominant groups toward minority groups in any country that has strong contemporary egalitarian values but discriminatory histories or policies. Despite its subtle expression, aversive racism has resulted

---

171  *CBS This Morning,* "CEO Mellody Hobson on Race in Corporate America and How to Create Change," June 24, 2020, video, 5:28.

172  John Dovidio et al, "Why Can't We Just Get Along? Interpersonal Biases and Interracial Distrust," *Cultural Diversity and Ethnic Minority Psychology* no. 8 (2002): 88-102.

in significant and pernicious consequences comparative to those of traditional, overt racism.[173]

## MICROAGGRESSIONS

Racial microaggressions are a common form of aversive racism. Psychologist Derald Wing Sue defines racial microaggressions as "brief and commonplace daily verbal, behavioral, or environmental indignities, whether intentional or unintentional, that communicate hostile, derogatory, or negative racial slights and insults toward people of color." Dr. Sue credits psychiatrist Chester Pierce with coining the term in the '70s.[174]

According to Dr. Sue, "Microaggressions hold their power because they are invisible, and therefore they don't allow us to see that our actions and attitudes may be discriminatory."[175] He goes on to say that microaggressions commonly are "everyday insults, indignities and demeaning messages sent to people of color by well-intentioned white people who are unaware of the hidden messages being sent to them." Unconscious actions such as snubs, looks, gestures, and tone in daily interactions can be damaging to the recipient. Dr. Sue said, "Microaggressions are detrimental to persons of color because they impair performance in a multitude of settings

---

173  John Dovidio and Samuel Gaertner, "Aversive Racism and Selection Decisions: 1989 and 1999," *Psychological Science* 11, no. 4 (July 2000): 315–319.

174  Derald Sue et al, "Racial Microaggressions in Everyday Life: Implications for Clinical Practice," *The American Psychologist* 62 no. 4 (2007): 271-286.

175  Tori DeAngelis, "Unmasking 'Racial Micro Aggressions,'" *American Psychological Association*, February 40 no. 2 (2009): 42.

by sapping the psychic and spiritual energy of recipients and by creating inequities."[176]

There are many different forms of microaggressions. Most commonly, they're verbal, behavioral, or environmental. A verbal microaggression could be a comment or question that stigmatizes a marginalized group of people, behavioral microaggressions happen when someone acts in a hurtful or discriminatory way, and environmental microaggressions are subtle discrimination within society.[177] Dr. Sue proposes a classification of racial microaggressions in three forms: microassault, microinsult, and microinvalidation.[178]

Microassaults are conscious, intentional, and overt forms of discrimination in which the perpetrator may not openly proclaim their biases.[179] Using racial slurs, displaying confederate flags or swastikas, or deliberately providing service to a white person before a person of color are all examples of microassaults.

Microinsults are statements or behaviors that subtly convey rudeness and insensitivity and demean a person's racial heritage or identity.[180] I've experienced this form of microaggression many times when a white person tells me, "You're so articulate!" I'm not sure what's more offensive—their

---

176  Sue et al, "Racial Microaggressions,"271-286.
177  Anna Smith, "What to Know About Microaggressions," Medical News Today, June 11, 2020, accessed July 25, 2020.
178  Sue et al, "Racial Microaggressions," 271-286.
179  Ibid.
180  Ibid.

surprise or the assumption that a highly educated African American woman can't speak standard English.

Microinvalidations are statements that deny, negate, or undermine the lived experiences of people of color. An examples of a microinvalidation could be a white person telling a person of color that racism doesn't exist or that reverse racism is real.[181]

Dr. Sue points out that microinsults and microinvalidiations are the most difficult to address because of their subtle nature, which can be particularly challenging for people of color. Recipients commonly feel insulted without knowing exactly why. In addition, the perpetrator is sometimes unaware that their words or actions are offensive. Dr. Sue wrote, "The person of color is caught in a Catch-22: If she confronts the perpetrator, the perpetrator will deny it."[182] Dr. Sue argues that this type of conundrum leaves the person of color questioning what actually happened, which often results in confusion and anger. Such interactions can also sap people of color's energy.

Kevin Nadal, a professor of psychology at John Jay College of Criminal Justice, believes addressing even small insults is important because microaggressions can have lasting impacts on a person' psyche. He explained, "Calling out microaggressions can be more productive than calling someone a racist." Dr. Sue agrees. "Microaggressions hold their power because they are invisible, and therefore they

---

181  Kevin Nadal, "A Guide to Responding to Microaggressions," CUNY Forum, accessed July 25, 2020.

182  Sue et al, "Racial Microaggressions,"271-286.

don't allow us to see that our actions and attitudes may be discriminatory."[183]


## STEREOTYPE THREAT

Stanford University psychology professor Claude Steele conducted research to examine the negative impacts stereotype threat can have on performance. Dr. Steele defines a stereotype threat as "being in a situation or doing something to which a negative stereotype about (an) identity is relevant." The research found that reminders that someone belongs to a stereotyped group, such as having to identify your race on standardized test, can have a negative impact on performance by members of a stereotyped group. When members of a minority group are exposed to a stereotype threat, they often achieve at a lower level than their non-minority counterparts. Dr. Steele has found that women in science, technology, engineering, and mathematics (STEM) as well as African American students are two groups that frequently encounter stereotype threat.[184]

Over three hundred published studies have validated Dr. Steele's research. Multiple studies have proved that stereotype threat is a primary reason for underperformance of minority groups in academic settings. The findings substantiate that when a student faces stereotype threat, the anxiety created by that negative assumption increases cognitive stress. Additionally, an individual's performance worsened when they

---

183 Tori DeAngelis, "Unmasking 'Racial Micro Aggressions'."
184 Claude Steele and Joshua Aronson, "Stereotype Threat and the Intellectual Test Performance of African-Americans," *Journal of Personality and Social Psychology* 62 no.1 (1995): 26-37.

are aware they may be judged on the basis of a negative stereotype. The impact is the same whether or not the individual believes the stereotype is true.[185] Stereotype threats and other microaggressions disproportionately impact Black women leaders. Our unique intersection of identities as women, people of color, and leaders can make us feel invisible in the workplace.

## THE INVISIBLE WOMAN

*I am invisible, understand, simply because people refuse to see me. Like the bodiless heads you see sometimes in circus sideshows, it is as though I have been surrounded by mirrors of hard, distorting glass. When they approach me they see only my surroundings, themselves or figments of their imagination, indeed, everything and anything except me.*[186]

—RALPH ELLISON, INVISIBLE MAN

Ralph Ellison's 1952 novel, *Invisible Man*, received the National Book Award in 1953 and is considered one of the most influential novels of the twentieth century. According to the *New York Times,* President Barack Obama modeled his memoir, *Dreams from My Father: A Story of Race and Inheritance,* after Ellison's novel.[187]

---

185  Caryn Block et al, "Contending with Stereotype Threat at Work: A Model of Long-Term Responses 1Ψ7," *The Counseling Psychologist* 39, no. 4 (May 2011): 570-600.

186  Ralph Ellison, *Invisible Man* (New York: Vintage International, 1995).

187  Greg Grandin, "Obama, Melville, and the Tea Party," *The New York Times,* January 18, 2014.

The narrator in *Invisible Man* is a nameless young Black man who takes the reader on a journey as he reflects on the various ways in which he has experienced social invisibility in his life. While Ellison wrote this novel decades ago, many Black people still feel invisible today. Unfortunately, no one is as invisible today as the Black woman. In my experience, there are certain things that leave me feeling invisible, such as a lack of eye contact even when I'm the most senior person in the meeting, not being invited to social gatherings, or having my comment or suggestion ignored only to have someone else—usually a white male—take credit for it.

In 2019, research from Catalyst found that women of color make up over 37 percent of women in the United States. Despite the significant number of women on color in the workforce, we hold only 18 percent of entry-level positions, few of which provide opportunities for advancement to leadership positions. Additionally, in 2019, women of color held 12 percent of managerial positions, 9 percent of senior managing and directing positions, 7 percent of vice presidential positions, 5 percent of senior vice presidential positions, and 4 percent of C-suite positions. Black women make up 13.7 percent of the population but only 1.3 percent of senior management and executive roles in S&P 500 companies and 2.2 percent in Fortune 500 boards of directors. Sadly, there's not one Black woman CEO of a Fortune 500 company.[188]

---

188 "Quick Take: Women of Color in the United States," Catalyst, March 19, 2020, accessed July 23, 2020.

Intersectional invisibility happens when people with multiple subordinate-group identities such as Black women don't fit the models of their respective identity groups.[189] Dr. Alexis Nicole Smith and her team of researchers spent seven years studying intersectional invisibility in a group of fifty-nine Black female senior leaders. The women in Dr. Smith's study reported feeling "physically visible yet cognitively invisible." One woman even said, "I'm the best choice for this job, and I'm probably not on your radar screen."[190]

As if invisibility weren't bad enough, a study in the *Journal of Experimental Social Psychology*

found that when organizations are failing, Black women leaders suffer double jeopardy: their supervisors evaluate them more negatively than Black men and white women in these situations. When an organization succeeds, however, supervisors evaluate each of these three groups similarly, but not quite as favorably as they do white men.[191]

University of Washington Tacoma social psychology professor Amanda Sesko's research is focused on the processes

---

189  Valerie Purdie-Vaughns and Richard Eibach, "Intersectional Invisibility: The Distinctive Advantages and Disadvantages of Multiple Subordinate-Group Identities," *Sex Roles* no. 59 (2008): 377–391.

190  Alexis Smith, "Interviews with 59 Black Female Executives Explore Intersectional Invisibility and Strategies to Overcome It," *Harvard Business Review,* May 10, 2018.

191  Ashleigh Rosette and Robert Livingston, "Failure is Not an Option for Black Women: Effects of Organizational Performance on Leaders with Single Versus Dual-Subordinate Identities," *Journal of Experimental Social Psychology* 48, no. 5 (2012): 1162-1167.

and outcomes of invisibility. She defines invisibility as "a unique form of discrimination that may be experienced by groups that do not fit race and gender prototypes—e.g., Black women."[192]

Dr. Sesko sees invisibility as a lack of individuation of or a lack of differentiation between group members, which supports that Black women from Dr. Smith's study say they go unnoticed or aren't recognized in their workplaces. Furthermore, Black women's voices often go unheard or their comments are misattributed to others more often than those of white women and Black and white men.[193]

## THE CONCRETE CEILING

Prior to pursuing a career in counseling psychology, Aisha Holder was a vice president at JPMorgan Chase's Corporate Training and Career Advancement Program. Now a psychologist at Columbia University, Dr. Holder uses her unique experiences as a Black woman who has navigated senior leadership roles in a large corporation in order to shine a light on the microaggressions and feelings of invisibility that impact Black women leaders. For example, she conducted a study of Black women leaders and found that coworkers and supervisors often perceive Black women as

---

192 Amanda Sesko and Monica Biernat, "Invisibility of Black Women: Drawing Attention to Individuality," *Group Processes & Intergroup Relations* 21, no. 1 (January 2018): 141–58.

193 Amanda Sesko and Monica Biernat, "Prototypes of Race and Gender: The Invisibility of Black Women," *Journal of Experimental Social Psychology,* 46 no.2 (2010), 356–360.

incapable of possessing the intelligence, savvy, and leadership abilities needed to excel in executive positions.[194]

Dr. Holder explained, "White women refer to a *glass ceiling* to describe barriers to career success whereas Black women encounter a *concrete ceiling*, whereby opportunities for career advancement are significantly reduced or nonexistent. The concrete ceiling is more challenging to penetrate as one cannot see through it." She also noted that Black women have a history of negative stereotypes, such as the "angry Black woman," which challenges their credibility and intellectual capabilities. As a result, they need to constantly prove themselves to their white colleagues. According to Dr. Holder, "These negative perceptions create a sense of invisibility and limit access to critical networks of influence in the workplace."[195]

## OVERQUALIFIED AND UNDERAPPRECIATED

As I think about microaggressions, the main one that comes to mind happened when I was a mid-level manager leading a small program office. At the time, I had already checked off a number of goals on my way to senior executive such as graduating from American University's Key Executive Program with a master's in Public Administration.[196] After the program, I realized I'd outgrown my job.

---

194 Aisha Holder, Margo Jackson, and Joseph Ponterotto, "Racial Microaggression Experiences and Coping Strategies of Black Women in Corporate Leadership," *Qualitative Psychology, 2* no.2, (2015): 164–180.

195 Ibid.

196 "About Key: Key Executive Leadership Programs," American University, accessed September 20, 2020.

During the fall of that year, the world had changed. On September 11, 2001, two hijacked planes hit the World Trade Center towers, one crashed in a Pennsylvania field, and another hit the Pentagon. I spent the next two months helping put the US air traffic control system back together. I volunteered to work in the crisis operations center, working nights, weekends, and holidays in a secure room sitting next to a very large Marine manning a red phone. After 9/11, I wanted to do something—anything—to help, so I temporarily gave up my comfortable day job in order to work in the FAA's emergency operations center. Taking on this new role gave me a sense of purpose during those dark post-9/11 days. When I returned to my old position a few months later, the itch to do something different grew even stronger.

I decided to apply for a promotion to a higher-level position with greater responsibility within another part of the air traffic organization for which I had worked after 9/11. I was qualified—more than qualified—for the recently vacated position. I had all the credentials, my master's degree, and all of the skills that you'd think would set me up for the next step of my career. I applied for the position and nailed the interview. In fact, after the interview, one of the panel members stopped me in the hallway and told me that I had "knocked it out of the park." The panelist also said that my interview was by far the best one and that I was the most qualified person for the job. They were sure I would be offered the position. Unfortunately, things didn't exactly turn out that way.

A couple of weeks went by before I got a call from our organization's top senior executive asking me to come to his office. To my surprise, he told me I didn't get the promotion. He then told me about the person who had been selected for the job. I was confused—the person selected didn't even meet the minimum qualifications in the job posting. He said they'd made an "exception" for this person, although never indicated that such a thing was possible. When I questioned this exception, the executive nervously changed the subject. He said he empathized with my disappointment, telling a rambling story about a time in his career when he was turned down for a promotion. He basically told me, "Get over it."

Long story short, the executive said the person who got the job had great technical skills. He selected him over me because, "It would take you me a couple of months to catch up on the technical details of the program." The problem with that excuse was that the position was a senior director with several layers of managers between the technical staff and the position itself. It was a leadership position, not a program manager's job.

The executive continued by saying that the selected candidate had strong technical skills and that I was "better with managing people." As if this conversation couldn't get any worse, he offered me the position of the selected candidate's deputy. He was clearly attempting to placate me with a job and cover up for the shortcomings of someone they'd hired who couldn't lead people. Worse still, I'd receive no promotion and no career advancement—I'd just end up supporting somebody who wasn't qualified to do the job.

In what I'm sure was a totally unrelated coincidence, the candidate who got the job also happened to be good friends with the senior boss—both of whom were white men.

I told the executive that I needed time to think. I left his office in a state of disbelief. I didn't get the job even though I was the most qualified candidate. Then, they wanted me to support the person they'd hired because he couldn't manage people. I'd be leading the organization without getting the title or the promotion. That night I talked with my most trusted adviser: my husband. I gave him a blow-by-blow description of the meeting. He simply asked me, "What do you want to do?" Did I want to file a complaint? We both knew that if I decided to pursue a complaint, I stood a good chance of winning. The question was, at what cost?

Sometimes winning a complaint is only a temporary victory, especially if that victory sidelines your career or traps you in a dead-end position. The answer to my husband's question was, "I'm done!" Over the next couple of weeks, I went in every day with a smile on my face as I planned my exit strategy. I told the boss that I didn't want to be this guy's permanent deputy. Instead, I agreed to a limited, temporary assignment as a way to buy time to figure out my next move.

After many hours of self-reflection and research, the planner in me came up with a strategy. I knew I wanted to continue building my resume and keep filling my leadership tool kit. The one glaring gap in my leadership resume was that I didn't have any experience working on Capitol Hill. While having Hill experience isn't a prerequisite for becoming a senior executive in the federal government, it's a significant differentiator. In addition, working on the Hill was something I really wanted to do. However, I had no desire to give up my good government job to take an entry level position just to get experience.

I found the Brookings LEGIS Fellows Program designed to give government leaders an opportunity to work on Capitol Hill. The two options that Brookings offered were a seven-month program and a one-year program. I knew that seven months wouldn't be long enough, so I decided to pursue the one-year program in order to experience the full legislative calendar.[197] With a plan in mind, I made an appointment to have a conversation with my boss. I told him that I had reflected on our last conversation and decided that I wanted developmental opportunities in order to be more competitive for the next promotion. I said, "Here's an opportunity for me to gain that last piece of the puzzle."

I handed him the announcement for the LEGIS Fellows program. The color drained from his face. He was speechless. I could only image what he was thinking. He could say no and run the risk of me filing a discrimination complaint or say yes to spending eight thousand dollars for my fellowship plus paying my salary for the year.[198] I said, "Let me give you a chance to think about it." I got up, walked out the door, and calmly went back to my desk. A few days later, he approved my request, and a month after that, I was a newly minted Brookings LEGIS fellow working on Capitol Hill.

Only years later could I assign a name for what happened to me: a microaggression. Executive coach Rania Anderson describes what happened to me as "same behavior, different description." She explains, "This type of microaggression occurs when people describe a woman's actions in ways

197 "WashU at Brookings," Brookings Institution, accessed September 20, 2020.

198 Ibid.

that would not be used to describe a man who did the same things."[199] How many white men would be denied a promotion for being "better at managing people?" My guess is none.

*Women in the Workplace 2018* found that 64 percent of working women have experienced microaggressions. The report found that "women have to provide more evidence of their competence than men and they have their judgment questioned in their area of expertise." The situation is even worse for women of color. "Black women, in particular, deal with a greater variety of microaggressions and are more likely than other women to have their judgment questioned in their area of expertise and be asked to provide additional evidence of their competence."[200]

I wish I could say that this example was the only time I experienced microaggressions in the workplace, but every new job or new assignment brings new challenges. The difference now is that I know how to spot microaggressions and confront them head on.

## COLOR BLIND OR COLOR BRAVE?

In a 2015 article in *Vanity* Fair magazine, Sheryl Sandberg, the former Facebook COO, credits a comment Mellody Hobson made for inspiring her to write her best-selling book, *Lean In.* "She [Mellody Hobson] said she wanted to be unapologetically black and unapologetically a woman," Sandberg

199 Rania Anderson, "5 Examples of Microaggressions in the Workplace," The Way Women Work, accessed September 20, 2020.
200 "Women in the Workplace 2018," LeanIn.Org and McKinsey & Company, October 2018, accessed September 20, 2020.

said. Although Sandberg isn't a Black woman, this comment helped her move past trying to make her womanhood fade into the background.

Mellody Hobson is also outspoken about race. Sandburg has said that despite the normally taboo subject of race, Hobson isn't afraid to bring it up. She "does and always did. She does it in such a way that people are able to hear it, and she does not mince words."[201]

When preparing for her TED Talk, Hobson remembered something her mother frequently asked her: "How did they treat you?" Her mother's haunting question, coupled with a story she read about a woman who would always tell her child to "be brave," gave her the idea for the talk, which she called "Color Blind or Color Brave?" During her talk, she challenges each of us: "Observe your environment. At work. At home. At school. And if you don't see any diversity, work to change it."[202]

### THE TAKEAWAYS

My journey as a Black woman in leadership has taken me through many challenging situations. I've experienced the loneliness of being the invisible woman and felt the sting of a thousand microaggressions. The subtilties of racism can sometimes make it hard to detect and even harder to fight.

Dr. Aisha Holder has developed coping strategies that Black women in corporate leadership can use to protect themselves

---

201 McLean, "Mellody Hobson."
202 Ibid.

against racial microaggressions. One such strategy is developing formal and informal networks to provide them with support, acceptance, and validation. She also found that self-empowerment is an adaptive behavior that can sustain a sense of self-worth. Many leaders also find strength in spirituality and in a deeply ingrained sense of purpose.[203]

I can attest that having a strong belief system can counteract the racial microaggressions I face in the workplace. I know who I am, what values I hold dear, and own my unique identity. When I lead with my identity, no one can make me feel invisible.

---

203 Holder, Jackson, and Ponterotto, "Racial Microaggression Experiences," 164–180.

## CHAPTER 9

# THE INTERSECTION OF LEADERSHIP AND IDENTITY

———

When you bring a complete and sure understanding of your identity to the leadership picture, you will stand out as a true leader who has much to offer. It's the marriage of identity and leadership that sets you apart as a twenty-first century leader.

—STEDMAN GRAHAM[204]

———

204 Steadman Graham, *Identity Leadership* (New York: Center Street, 2019) 41.

For many of us, parts of our identity such as our gender, race, and ethnicity are always on display. Other parts like our religion, sexual orientation, education, or socioeconomic background may be harder to discern.205 We're all multidimensional, complex creatures who see the world in distinct ways. Saying someone is just like someone else discounts the importance of viewing each other as unique individuals. Short-sighted stereotyping can be especially hazardous for leaders at all levels.

## WHO YOU ARE IS WHO YOU ARE

*Who you are is who you are. If you cannot be who you are where you are, you change where you are not who you are*
.  —CAROLINE WANGA[206]

Caroline Wanga has been shattering stereotypes of what a successful Fortune 500 executive looks like. First of all, her style is unconventional for an executive. In Shellie Karabell's article about fashion for busines women in *Forbes Magazine*, she said, "40-something women leaders today project an image that is both appealing and powerful, strong but not overbearing, confident but not arrogant. As any businessman would want to be."[207] Karabell would probably frown upon

---

205 Shahram Heshmat, "What Do We Mean by Identity and Why Does Identity Matter?" *Science of Choice* (blog), *Psychology Today,* December 8, 2014.

206 *The Forum on Workplace Inclusion,* "Caroline Wanga, VP Diversity and Inclusion - Target Corporation," May 19, 2016, video, 3:33.

207 Shellie Karabell, "Dressing Like A Leader: Style Tips For Women In The Spotlight," *Forbes Magazine*, January 16, 2016, accessed September 20, 2020.

Wanga's bright red hair that's braided into a top knot. She also wears regal, brightly colored African prints and bold eyewear that seems more in line with an artist than with her position in the C-suite. Wanga truly embodies one of her favorite sayings: "Who you are is non-negotiable."

This mindset seems to have benefitted Wanga. From 2015 until 2020, she was chief culture, diversity & inclusion officer and vice president of human resources for the Target Corporation. Target is the eighth largest retailer in the United States, employs over 360,000 people, and rakes in revenue in excess of $70 billion per year.[208]

Caroline Wanga's identity journey began in Kenya. She says she grew up in a place where everyone looked like her and she believes that she's the product of other people's positive and empowering voices. She left Kenya and immigrated to Minnesota with her parents, both of whom have PhDs. After dropping out of college her freshman year when she became pregnant with her daughter, Cadence, Wanga spent seven years as a community organizer working with nonprofit organizations. She then returned to college, graduating with a bachelor's degree in business administration from Texas College. In 2005, Wanga began her Target career as a supply chain intern. She served in a variety of transformational leadership roles at Target, including supply chain, business intelligence, digital, and strategy capabilities, before joining the diversity and inclusion team in 2014.[209]

---

208 Ellen McGirt, "Target's Caroline Wanga Is Here to Change the World," *Fortune Magazine,* October 10, 2019.

209 Ellen McGirt and Jessica Helfand, "S7E1: Caroline Wanga," October 8, 2019, in *The Design of Business | The Business of Design*, podcast, 34:28.

Wanga developed her leadership skills early in her Target career. She gained experience managing large teams and learned operations and leadership skills that serve her to this day. Landing a role in diversity and inclusion (D & I) was like returning to her roots. She said, "D & I felt like community organizing." One of the first things she did in her new role was set up town halls to provide an opportunity for the Target workforce to express their concerns. Through the town halls, she developed "courageous listening," which she describes as listening to someone else's perspectives without feeling pressure to change your own personal narrative.[210]

Target netted tangible business results from Wanga's efforts. Three years after putting in the role of chief culture, diversity & inclusion officer, Target met seven of eight major diversity goals that the company established. Her innovative shared-accountability approach to driving business results was featured in *The Innovation Mentality* by Glenn Llopis, *Our Search for Belonging* by Howard Ross, and *The Multiplier Effect of Inclusion* by Dr. Tony Byers."[211] Additionally, "It's the first time Target ever had enterprise goals tied to philanthropy, product marketing, and supplier diversity owned by the business leaders," Wanga said. Brian Cornell, chairman and CEO of Target, can attest to Wanga's impact on the enterprise. "Caroline's contributions have been significant, and she championed our approach to diversity and inclusion and built a leading strategy that drove measurable and meaningful results across the enterprise."[212]

---

210 McGirt, "Caroline Wanga."
211 "2018 Religious Diversity Leadership Summit Bios," Tanenbaum Center for Interreligious Understanding, accessed September 20, 2020.
212 McGirt and Helfand, "Caroline Wanga."

Wanga may not have had the same groundbreaking career without some self-reflection. Just before her transition to D & I, Wanga suffered a personal crisis. She fell into a deep depression and sought help to recover. She said the depression was the result of "carrying the burden of being someone else for too long." This realization liberated her and allowed her to express who she really was, beginning with how she dressed. She gave up suits and cardigans and started wearing the African fabrics and hairstyles that represented her Kenyan heritage.[213]

Wanga sees the traditional African attire as "a way to be my ancestor's wildest dreams." She declares that she will never be the conventional businesswoman. She said, "I show up as me so I can never go back to being stuck." While dressing differently may mean she isn't welcome in some venues, she's willing to stand by her right to be unique. "The where's that I show up in are the where's that are comfortable with who I am."[214]

You can't show up on the first day of working expecting the culture to change to suit you. Wanga tells emerging leaders they must earn the right to show their uniqueness in the workplace. "Authenticity in the workplace doesn't exist if you don't have a workplace. Living your authentic self can never be an excuse for not doing your job well." She continues, "The first step in building your foundation is to do your job and do it well." The next step is to build strategic relationships with people who witness your strong work ethic and can vouch for you when assignments and promotions are being

213  Ibid.

214  *Management Leadership for Tomorrow, "Authenticity: Who You are is Non-Negotiable,"* April 29, 2020, video, 37:16.

decided. With a strong foundation in place, "You can begin to sprinkle in your authentic self by bringing forward your unique perspective and intrusive insights."[215]

Caroline Wanga practices what she preaches. "It's important for me to model what I'm asking people to do because there is real fear in bringing your authenticity to work, whatever that means for you."[216] Her authenticity and uniqueness helped her became the interim CEO for Essence Communications, one of the leading Black-owned communications technology companies, in the summer of 2020.

## IDENTITY AT THE CROSSROADS: THE INTERSECTION OF RACE AND GENDER

Issues of identity are never simple and can often be challenging to navigate, partly because most of us hold multiple identities. One of the identities I hold is being a Black woman. As a result, I've faced discrimination because of my race, at other times because of my gender, and occasionally because of being both Black and a woman—a double-edged sword. The concept of having overlapping identities and facing various levels of discrimination because of them is known as intersectionality.[217]

According to Merriam-Webster Dictionary, intersectionality is "used to refer to the complex and cumulative way that the effects

---

215   Ibid.
216   "About," Caroline A. Wanga, accessed September 9, 2020.
217   Merrill Perman, "The Origin of the Term 'Intersectionality'," *Language Corner* (blog), *Columbia Journalism Review*, October 23, 2018.

of different forms of discrimination (such as racism, sexism, and classism) combine, overlap, and yes, intersect—especially in the experiences of marginalized people or groups."[218]

Kimberlé Crenshaw, a professor at Columbia University Law School, director of the Center for Intersectionality and Social Policy Studies, and co-founder of the African American Policy Forum, first coined the term "intersectionality" in 1989. Crenshaw first used the term in a paper as a way to help explain the oppression of African American women. In recent years, the concept of intersectionality has gained traction in national conversations about racial justice, identity politics, and policing.[219]

Professor Crenshaw believes that "intersectionality is a lens through which you can see where power comes and collides, where it interlocks and intersects. It's not simply that there's a race problem here, a gender problem here, and a class or LGBTQ problem there. Many times, that framework erases what happens to people who are subject to all of these things."[220] Crenshaw has also witnessed the implications of intersectionality in connection to her experience as part of the 1991 legal team for Anita Hill, the woman who accused then-US Supreme Court Nominee Clarence Thomas of sexual harassment.

In Professor Crenshaw's 2016 TED Talk, "The urgency of intersectionality," which has over 1.7 million views, she described how

218 *Merriam-Webster.com Dictionary*, s.v. "Intersectionality," accessed September 10, 2020.
219 Perman, "Intersectionality.
220 Ibid.

she became interested in the idea of intersectionality. She told the story of an African American woman who filed a lawsuit against a factory for hiring discrimination. The woman claimed that the factory didn't hire her because she is a Black woman. The judge dismissed her case because the company hired Black men and white women, therefore she couldn't prove discrimination. However, just because the factory hired Black men and white women didn't mean they hired Black women. At the time of this case, the law didn't have a way to recognize the intersection of race and gender in discrimination cases.[221]

The theory of intersectionality may have originally started with Sojourner Truth, an African American abolitionist and women's rights activist.[222] She escaped slavery in 1826, became a Christian, and preached about abolitionism and equal rights for all. She continued her crusade for the rest of her life, earning an audience with President Abraham Lincoln and becoming one of the world's best-known human rights crusaders. She is most famous for her speech on racial inequalities, "Ain't I a Woman?" In this speech, which she delivered extemporaneously at the 1851 Ohio Women's Rights Convention, Truth argued that differential treatment based on gender or race didn't adequately capture the struggles she encountered as a result of the overlap of her gender and race throughout her life.[223]

221 *TED,* "The Urgency of Intersectionality | Kimberlé Crenshaw," December 7, 2016, video, 18:49.

222 Avtar Brah and Ann Phoenix, "Ain't I A Woman? Revisiting Intersectionality," *Journal of International Women's Studies* 5 vol. 3 (2004): 75-86.

223 Pat McKissack, *Sojourner Truth: Ain't I a Woman? 1944-2017* (New York: Scholastic, 1992).

## IT'S LONELY AT THE TOP

Twenty-first century women of color still aren't immune to intersectional discrimination. "I think about this all the time," said Stacy Brown-Philpot, the chief executive of TaskRabbit. "When I get on stage, I'm a black woman. And I'm a black C.E.O. Being a C.E.O. in general can be lonely sometimes. As one of the few black female C.E.O.s, the loneliness builds." The *Women in the Workplace 2019* annual report confirms the loneliness of being the only woman and woman of color.[224]

Brown-Philpot's road from being raised by a single mother in Detroit to commanding a boardroom in Silicon Valley is inspirational. She graduated from the University of Pennsylvania's Wharton School of Business, worked as an accountant at a major accounting firm, became an investment banker at Goldman Sachs, then went on to earn a graduate degree from Stanford University's Graduate School of Business. She joined Google in 2003, where Sheryl Sandberg became her mentor. While at Google, she assumed a series of leadership roles and founded the Black Googlers Network, an employee resource group. After nine years at Google, Brown-Philpot left to become COO of TaskRabbit—a technology company that pairs freelancers with people seeking help with odd jobs— and in 2016, she became CEO. She has since sold the company to Ikea, the Swedish furniture giant.[225]

Brown-Philpot's feelings of loneliness and isolation are common for women of color. Catalyst studied the emotional tax

---

224 Rachel Thomas et al, *Women in the Workplace 2019*, Lean In and McKinsey & Company, 2019.

225 David Gelles, "Stacy Brown-Philpot of TaskRabbit on Being a Black Woman in Silicon Valley," *New York Times*, July 13, 2018.

that both women and men of color face in the workplace. "It's a feeling of having to protect against bias or unfair treatment—of having to be on guard," said Dnika J. Travis, vice president of research for Catalyst. The survey of almost 1,600 participants in a variety of corporate and noncorporate settings included those who identified as Asian, African American, Latino, or a combination of any of those. Almost 58 percent said they were highly on guard at work. Women of color were slightly more worried about racial bias at work than sexism.[226]

The emotional tax is not just a phenomenon of corporate America. Yung-Yi Diana Pan, assistant professor of sociology at Brooklyn College, said, "As a woman of color, students often challenge us in a way they don't challenge their male professors, especially their white male professors."[227]

Stacy Brown-Philpot is making it her mission to change the landscape of Silicon Valley, starting with TaskRabbit. She explained, "I'm focusing on changing the face of technology by creating a diverse company where people feel they can bring their whole selves to work." TaskRabbit has demonstrated that commitment. Sixty percent of the company's leadership is women, 48 percent of its employees are Hispanic, African American, Asian, or two or more races, and 16 percent identify as LGBTQ.[228]

---

226 Dnika J. Travis, Jennifer Thorpe-Moscon, and Courtney McCluney, "Emotional Tax: How Black Women and Men Pay More at Work and How Leaders Can Take Action," Catalyst, 2016.

227 Ibid.

228 Jessica Guynn, "TaskRabbit Teams with Black Lawmakers to Boost Tech Diversity," USA Today, April 23, 2016.

## CODE-SWITCHING

Code-switching is the process of shifting from one language or dialect to another depending on the social setting. It's used as a way for members of minority or ethnic groups to fit in with the broader majority community while maintaining connections with their identity.[229]

Code-switching for native speakers who switch seamlessly back and forth between Spanish and English is also called "Chicano English" or "Spanglish."[230] Many African Americans code-switch between Standard American English and African American Vernacular English or Ebonics, a dialect widely spoken by Americans of African descent.[231]

Code-switching is an important component of identity for many people of color. In 2013, Gene Demby started a podcast on NPR called *Code Switch*. Demby explained the connection between language and culture: "We're hop-scotching between different cultural and linguistic spaces and different parts of our own identities—sometimes within a single interaction."[232]

Code switching is a facet of my life as a woman of color. The parts of my identity I display with close friends and family are different from who I am when I'm running a large

229 *Encyclopaedia Britannica Online,* s.v. "Code-Switching," by Carlos D. Morrison, accessed July 11, 2020.
230 *TEDx Talks,* "Spanglish is a Language Too: Alondra Posada," video, June 27, 2018, 6:16.
231 *Encyclopaedia Britannica Online,* s.v. "Ebonics," by Salikoko Sangol Mufwene, accessed July 11, 2020.
232 Gene Demby, "How Code-Switching Explains The World," *Code Switch* (blog), *NPR,* April 8, 2013.

organization or speaking in front of a predominantly white male audience. When I'm with family and close friends, I can easily slip into the vernacular of my Southern roots. I've been known to drop a "g" or use contractions that are not found in Merriam-Webster's dictionary. I might say, "I'm fix'ta go to the store, y'all need anything?" At work, I would probably reframe it. I would say, "I'm headed to Starbucks. Can I get you anything?" I can code switch with the best of them.

Former President Barack Obama is the king of code-switching. He seamlessly moves from the eloquent prose of statesmanship to rhythmic conversations on the basketball court. At the lunch counter of the iconic Ben's Chili Bowl in Washington, DC, an observer saw Obama conversing with locals and members of his staff. A Black cashier asked him if the needed any change, to which President Obama replied, "Nah, we straight."[233] President Obama may switch up his vernacular, but his values remain the same no matter the audience.

Ida Harris wrote about her experiences with code-switching in an opinion piece for YES! Magazine. She interviewed Dr. Dionne Mahaffey, an Atlanta-based business psychologist and coach, who admitted that code-switching can be draining but that it's also a beneficial part of the Black experience. Dr. Mahaffey explained, "Code-switching does not employ an inauthentic version of self, rather, it calls upon certain aspects of our identity in place of others, depending on the space or circumstance. It's exhausting because we can actually feel the difference." Harris concluded, "I realize that code-switching, for some, is not about assimilating but

---

233 Ibid.

surviving."[234] For me, code-switching is another tool in my toolkit. I've learned to use it as a way to connect the various parts of my identity.

## KEY TAKEAWAYS

Michelle Obama said, "There's power in allowing yourself to be known and heard, in owning your unique story, in using your authentic voice. And there's grace in being willing to know and hear others."[235] One of the primary lessons of leadership is to embrace who you are in order to be able to allows others to bring their best selves to work.

My personal identity is the vessel that contains the essence of who I am. I see the world through the lens of the various identities I hold. The number of identities changes with every new experience or relationship that develops. The person I am today contains traces of who I was as a young girl, the woman I've grown into, and the dreams of who I will be. It also carries the DNA of my ancestors.

Like Caroline Wanga, my journey to discover my authentic self has taken me to some wonderful places and some not so wonderful places. I've earned the right to show my authenticity and to recognize when who I am doesn't fit. Learning to recognize where it's safe to sprinkle my authenticity and where to keep it in my pocket has been one of the best lessons I've learned.

---

234  Ida Harris, "Code-Switching Is Not Trying to Fit in to White Culture, It's Surviving It," *YES! Magazine,* December 17, 2019, accessed July 12, 2020.

235  Michelle Obama, *Becoming* (New York: Random House, 2018).

## CHAPTER 10

# OWNING YOUR NARRATIVE

—

To wake the giant inside ourselves, we have
to be faithful to our own eccentric nature
and bring it out into conversation with
the world.

−DAVID WHYTE[236]

Brené Brown knows a thing or two about owning your
story. In *Rising Strong*, she said, "Owning our stories means
acknowledging our feelings and wrestling with the hard
emotions—our fear, anger, aggression, shame, and blame.
This isn't easy, but the alternative—denying our stories and
disengaging from emotion—means choosing to live our

---

236 David Whyte, *Crossing the Unknown Sea: Work As a Pilgrimage of
Identity* (New York: Riverhead Books, 2001), 51.

entire lives in the dark. It means no accountability, no learning, no growth."[237]

Every rung you ascend up the leadership ladder requires less and less of what you know. The climb demands less knowledge and more knowing. Warren Bennis, one of the world's most influential scholars on the subject of leadership, said, "Becoming a leader is synonymous with becoming yourself. It is precisely that simple and it is also that difficult."[238] In order to ascend, you must know who you are, what matters most, and why you decided to step into the arena. What's pulling you? What drives you forward when it would be easier to rest in comfort? For the sake of what cause, mission, or purpose are you climbing ever higher?

To understand where we're headed, we need to understand the current landscape and the role identity plays into leadership. Our identities are based on a complex mix of characteristics such as race, gender, sexuality, class, religion, and nationality. University of Washington professor Anu Taranath wrote, "The ways in which all of these various categories intersect with and inform our individual lives creates the uniqueness of each of us."[239]

Many elements comprise a person's identity, and these elements relate to what makes us who we are as humans. Some

---

237 Brené Brown, *Rising Strong* (New York: Spiegel & Grau, an imprint of Random House, 2015).

238 Warren Bennis, *On Becoming a Leader* (Cambridge, MA: Perseus Pub, 2003).

239 Anu Taranath, "Difference, Identity and Power," Washington University Office of Minority Affairs, accessed July 12, 2020.

of these elements are a choice and others we are born with or have no control over. For most of us, our race and ethnicity play a significant role in how we see ourselves, especially if we feel that we are different from the majority of those who live and work in our community.

Your purpose is your story. The journey is the narrative of your life. It's time to stop living out someone else's fantasy and take the pen. You'll never be happy or truly successful until you write your own story. No one else can do it for you.

## MAPPING YOUR IDENTITY

Who would've thought I would make peace with my identity at a coaches' conference? I certainly didn't expect to discover deeper meaning on a beautiful, crisp fall day. On the drive from my home to the conference hotel in suburban Washington, DC, all I could focus on was the hellish traffic and the stack of paperwork waiting for me on my desk. As I parked in the garage, I took a deep breath and headed into what I thought would be another round of death by PowerPoint.

Spending the day sitting outside enjoying the clear blue skies would've been nice. I remember thinking, "It's too nice to be cooped up in a small room, baking under the glow of fluorescent lights." However, a day in the sunshine wasn't in the cards for me. I had work to do. I would be introducing two workshops that day. The first was a session on identity mapping.

Social identity is a person's sense of pride and self-esteem derived from the groups they belong to. As humans, we tend to see the world as "us" or "them," or as "in-groups" and "out-groups." In the late 1970s, Henri Tajfel, a noted social psychologist, developed the Social Identity Theory that explains the underlying drivers for prejudice and social identity. He proposed that stereotyping—putting people into groups and categories—is based on a normal cognitive process.[240]

Tajfel explains, "The brain has a propensity to group things together in ways that tend to exaggerate the differences between groups and emphasizes the similarities of things in the same group." The central hypothesis of Social Identity Theory is that members of an in-group will seek to find negative aspects of an out-group, thus enhancing their self-image.[241] We all categorize people in the same way—some to a larger extent than others. Social categorization of people is one explanation for prejudices that can, in turn, lead to racism.

In addition to social identity, everyone has an ethnic identity as well. We use these selected cultural and sometimes physical characteristics to classify people into groups or categories. According to social psychologist Peter Weinreich, one's ethnic identity is "made up of those dimensions that express the continuity between one's construal of past ancestry and one's future aspirations in relation to ethnicity."[242]

240 Henri Tajfel and John C. Turner, "The Social Identity Theory of Intergroup Behavior," *Political Psychology* (January 9, 2004): 276–293.
241 Ibid.
242 Peter Weinreich and Wendy Saunderson, *Analysing Identity: Cross-Cultural, Societal, and Clinical Contexts* (London: Routledge, 2003), 80.

Identity was something with which I had been struggling all my life. This session gave me an opportunity to try to make some sense of who I was and where I fit in. The premise of the workshop, "Social Identity Coaching Lab," was interesting because it assumed that each of us carries around a number of different identities that act as the lens through which we see the world. Mona Khan and Peter Godard facilitated this workshop.[243] I instantly determined that the Social Identity Coaching Lab wasn't your typical conference event.

Mona began by introducing herself. She said, "Welcome to the Social Identity Coaching Lab! My name is Mona. I'm a woman of color, Gen X-er, South Asian, cisgender, heterosexual, and a 'third culture kid.'"[244] At first glance, I would have never thought all of those identities belonged to the short, wiry, fair-skinned woman in front of me. Her short-bobbed hair, glasses, and conservative business suit stood in stark contrast to the vibrant, multifaceted identities she holds.

Social Identity Mapping is a way to visually represent and understand an individual's network of group memberships. This exercise helps you identify the groups to which you believe you belong and determine the importance you place on being a part of those groups. It's a great exercise to help teams understand each individual's identity and to see where there are similarities or differences.[245]

---

243 "Capital Coaches Conference Agenda," ICF Metro DC, accessed July 13, 2020.

244 Ibid.

245 Tegan Cruwys et al, "Social Identity Mapping: A Procedure for Visual Representation and Assessment of Subjective Multiple Group Memberships," *The British Journal of Social Psychology* 55 no. 4 (2016): 613-642.

Mona demonstrated the power of the Social Identity Mapping Tool during the workshop.[246] She walked us through the process of unpacking all of the different identities we carry around within us. She also showed us how misconceptions about other races and genders can lead to conflict. I learned that the identities I carry inside not only impact how I see myself, but also how I see others—everyone can be biased toward those we view as different. One of the greatest lessons from this exercise was comparing how each participant's individual map compared with that of others. I was amazed seeing the overlapping identities between people whose external appearances seemed so diverse, which shows we're all more alike than we are different.

I left the workshop feeling like a flower opening up to expose different parts of myself. I learned that identity isn't about feeling less than or unwelcome. If we recognize the unique identities each of us possess, we can unlock our true potential and creativity.

After this life-changing workshop, I wanted to know more about Mona and her journey of finding her identity. A few months later, I asked her for an interview.

### THE WATERS IN WHICH I SWAM
Mona's journey started in the Philippines and toggled back and forth between the United States, Europe, and Asia. She recounted that she grew up in places where most people came

---

246 Sarah Bentley et al, "Social Identity Mapping Online, *Journal of Personality and Social Psychology* 118 no. 2 (2020): 213–241.

from somewhere else—places in which people of different ethnicities, cultures, and religions coexisted. In her world, there were many people of color in positions of authority. She had plenty of role models who helped her navigate life. She said, "In the waters in which I swam, everyone had a passport."

When Mona started graduate school in Minnesota, she became acutely aware that she was different, even though there were a large number of refugee communities represented in the university population. She found that most people were very friendly; she still didn't feel like she fit in. She explained, "I did fine, I did well, but never quite felt like I would be understood. I would often get a lot of, 'Oh, that's very interesting,' which was code for that's odd." Mona admitted she may have been blind to the diversity of identities within Minnesota because it felt very white, even though many in the community believed themselves to be progressive. What really struck her was that this liberal community had little diversity yet sought to be so inclusive. However, she never was able to shake the feeling of otherness, so she left Minnesota and relocated to Washington, DC, after graduation.

Mona's experiences living in six countries and working with people of diverse identities, experiences, and perspectives led her to focus on helping people connect across differences in an increasingly complex world. Mona has a bachelor's degree in political science and economics from Sarah Lawrence College and the London School of Economics, and she earned her master's as a MacArthur Scholar from the University of Minnesota's Hubert H. Humphrey Institute of Public Affairs.

Mona is also a graduate of Georgetown University's Institute for Transformational Leadership and she is a certified leadership coach.[247]

Mona's exploration of identity blossomed as she worked in consulting and nonprofit organizations early in her career. She was attracted to activists like Audre Lorde, the award-winning writer and poet whose work is deeply intersectional. Lorde said, "Certainly there are very real differences between us.... But it is not those differences between us that are separating us. It is rather our refusal to recognize those differences."[248]

Mona believes that having a clear sense of who we are is the anchor that sustains us in the face of a world that doesn't always value people who are different. She's definitely true to her values. She said, "I have a clear sense of who I am and a clear sense of self definition. I did not have the feeling, 'I'm less than.' I had the feeling, 'This context doesn't quite suit me. These are not the waters in which I want to swim." Mona added, "I think that this clarity about exploration and about identity allowed me not to internalize this feeling of otherness in a way that could erode my confidence."

For the past eighteen years, Mona has worked with activists, foundations, and nonprofit organizations to promote the rights and welfare of women, youth, LGBTQ people, immigrants, refugees, internally displaced persons, indigenous populations, and workers. Mona later founded the Social Identity Lab and developed the Social Identity Mapping Tool, which

---

247 Chiron Strategic, "Bios."
248 "Audre Lorde," Writing on Glass (blog), accessed July 13, 2020.

allows the participant to create a personal identity map that resembles concentric circles in a tree.[249] These identity maps can be used in a number of different ways around equity and inclusion work since they help people identify not only their differences, but also how much they have in common.

Mona believes that knowledge is power. Ultimately, she wants to support others to harness knowledge—be it self-awareness, clarity about what stands in the way of accomplishment, or a road map for the future to build a better world. She stays true to who she is and listens to her father's voice in her head saying, "Remember where you come from." That sense of knowing where she came from continues to anchor her. The connection to her identity replenishes her reservoir and keeps her moving through turbulent waters.

## BE THE AUTHOR OF YOUR STORY

There are six main steps you can follow to take control of the narrative of your life and help you own your identity.

### STEP ONE: LET GO OF THE "NOTS."

Most of us have a chorus of negative thoughts playing in the background of our daily lives. As a Black woman, my choir told me, "You're not good enough," "You're not smart enough," and "You're not one of the in-crowd." Fortunately, I've learned to replace these "nots" with affirmations that help me to celebrate who I am: "I am worthy, I am powerful, and I am enough!"

---

249 Chiron Strategic, "Bios."

**STEP TWO: APPRECIATE YOUR STRENGTHS.**

What can you do better than anyone else? What are your God-given abilities? What are the things that your friends, family, and colleagues look to you to provide? What are the talents that light you up and get you excited? Who are you on your best days? What's your superpower? There's power in writing things down; the *Journal of Experimental Psychology* published research that confirms writing down your thoughts can reduce intrusive thoughts about negative events and improve working memory.[250] The act of writing something down signals to your brain that what's being written is important. Journaling is a powerful tool that helps you focus on your strengths.

**STEP THREE: CONSIDER THE WORDS YOU USE TO DESCRIBE YOURSELF AND YOUR ACHIEVEMENTS.**

Beware of the qualifiers—they can be deadly to the spirit. "Kind of," "a little," "some," and "except for" can kill a dream before it starts. Qualifiers can get in the way of your achieving the full measure of success because they diminish your true talents and make you hesitate to step into your greatness. I used to turn these deadly weapons on myself to minimize my dreams and hide my light. Once I stopped the "kinda, sorta" thinking about my value and strengths, I started to step into my identity. There's true power in letting yourself think bigger. I discovered the weapon to neutralize the qualifiers: awareness. You can't change what you don't notice. Notice every time you use qualifiers in

---

250  Kitty Klein and Adriel Boals, "Expressive Writing Can Increase Working Memory Capacity," *Journal of Experimental Psychology* 130 no.3 (September 2001):520-33.

your thoughts and in your utterances. Noticing them gives you the opportunity to reframe the thought and eliminate the qualifiers.

### STEP FOUR: EMBRACE YOUR JOURNEY UP UNTIL NOW.

Take the time to explore some of the crucible moments in your life. A crucible moment is a transformative experience that changes you in a significant way. You can recognize those crucibles and emerge from them with a new perspective on life and new layers of your identity.[251] Spend time journaling about pivotal moments in your life. What did you learn about yourself? What strengths emerged and what may have gotten in the way? How did it change you? What did you do with what you learned? Being willing to look at your past takes courage, but as Brené Brown said, "When we have the courage to walk into our story and own it, we get to write the ending."[252]

### STEP FIVE: FIGURE OUT THE RECIPE FOR YOUR SECRET SAUCE.

Use your history, your identity, and your strengths to extract the ingredients or characteristics that make you great. Notice how I didn't say good or okay. I said great. To own your story, you must own your greatness. I'm sure you call rattle off a litany of weaknesses and areas of deficiency. For most of us, naming our strengths is hard. Take some time to embody

---

251  Warren Bennis and Robert Thomas, "Crucibles of Leadership," *Harvard Business Review* (September 2002):39-45.

252  Brené Brown, *Daring Greatly: How the Courage to Be Vulnerable Transforms the Way We Live, Love, Parent and Lead* (New York: Penguin Random House 2013).

what makes you shine on your best days. If you're struggling to identify your superpowers, spend time figuring out what's getting in the way. This exercise is a great way to include your trusted circle of friends and mentors in the process. Ask them what stands out about you and what it is that you do better than anyone else. Write it down. Own it.

**STEP SIX: DRAFT THE NEXT CHAPTER IN YOUR STORY.**
Start with the following questions: who could you be if you let go of fear? What's the worst that could happen? What's the best that could happen? What's getting in the way? I encourage you to dream big. If that dream doesn't scare you, it's not big enough! What's the one big thing that will help launch you? The hardest part is to follow Stephen Covey's advice: begin with the end in mind.[253]

Having a compelling personal vision of the future is an essential part of taking command of your story. Richard Boyatzis, noted author, researcher, and expert in the field of emotional intelligence and behavior change, found that "a personal vision based on an ideal self is required if the vision is to lead to sustained and desired change."[254]

253 Stephen Covey, *The 7 Habits of Highly Effective People: Restoring the Character Ethic* (New York: Free Press, 2004).
254 Richard Boyatzis, et al, "The Role of the Positive Emotional Attractor in Vision and Shared Vision: Toward Effective Leadership, Relationships, and Engagement," *Frontiers in Psychology* 670 vol. 6 (May 21, 2015).

## KEY TAKEAWAYS

In the past, I ran away from issues of diversity and inclusion. Bigotry and sexism are threads in my story, and succeeding in spite of overt and covert racism is an important piece of my testimony. My narrative is my legacy. I'm leaving footprints for others to follow just as we are walking in the footprints left by our ancestors. There are times when we can use them as guideposts to direct our way.

There comes a time when each of us must chart our own course, divert from the well-trodden path, and follow our destiny. Our new path leaves footprints for our progeny to follow. In turn, they will divert from the trail we leave behind and find their own way. If we do our jobs well, they'll have the tools they need to succeed.

## FINALLY, REMEMBER THE STEPS FOR EMBRACING YOUR TRUE IDENTITY AND OWNING YOUR NARRATIVE:

1. Let go of the "nots."
2. Appreciate your strengths.
3. Consider the words you use—beware of the qualifiers.
4. Embrace your journey up until now.
5. Figure out the recipe for your secret sauce.
6. Draft the next chapter in your story.

# PART THREE

# THE MAKING OF A LEADER

# CHAPTER 11

# THE INNER CRITIC

—

The voice of "not-me"—the internal
chatter that tells a woman that she's not
ready to lead, she's not enough of an
expert, she's not good enough for this
or that. It's the voice of self-doubt, of the
inner critic. We begin our journey here
because it is what most holds women
back from playing big.

−TARA MOHR[255]

Many successful women, while polished and accomplished
on the outside, feel like impostors on the inside. The itty-bitty
committee in their heads that represents their inner critic
keeps up a constant refrain of doubts and insecurities. That

---

255  Tara Mohr, *Playing Big: Practical Wisdom for Women Who Want to
Speak Up, Create, and Lead* (New York: Avery, 2015).

inner dialogue can sabotage your confidence, no matter how many accolades you receive. There's a name for this experience: impostor syndrome.

## IMPOSTOR SYNDROME

Impostor syndrome is a condition that approximately 70 percent of us will experience during our lifetime. It's so pervasive that a recent Google search for "Impostor syndrome" yielded nearly three million hits.[256] If you're like me, you may have felt the sting of impostor syndrome at a time when you reached a career milestone or won a prestigious award. No matter how many times you're lauded for great achievements, there's always a voice that says you don't deserve it.[257]

Georgia State University psychologists Pauline Clance and Suzanne Imes discovered impostor syndrome in 1978. Their study, "The Imposter Phenomenon in High Achieving Women: Dynamics and Therapeutic Intervention," is still viewed as the definitive data source on the subject.

Dr. Clance became interested in impostor syndrome while in graduate school. Taking exams would fill her with dread. She said, "I remembered all I did not know rather than what I did. My friends began to be sick of my worrying, so I kept my doubts more to myself."[258]

---

256 Jaruwan Sakulku and James Alexander, "The imposter phenomenon," *International Journal of Behavioral Science* 6 no. 1 (2011):73-92.
257 Pauline Rose Clance, "Imposter Phenomenon," accessed June 23, 2020.
258 Ibid.

As a college professor at a prestigious liberal arts college, Dr. Clance heard similar stories from her students. She recalled one of her students saying, "I feel like an impostor here with all these really bright people." Dr. Clance's discussions with Dr. Imes about the common fears she shared with these students led to the concept of "Impostor Phenomenon." Impostor syndrome or impostorism is a psychological pattern in which one doubts one's accomplishments and has a persistent internalized fear of being exposed as a fraud.[259] In most instances, the person really is competent. However, those experiencing this phenomenon remain convinced that they're frauds and don't deserve all they have achieved.

I can attest to the destructive nature of impostor syndrome. There have been times in my life when my goal was to blend in. The truth is, I rarely fit in and quite frequently I'm the only person in the room who looks like me. I am a Black woman navigating spaces that are predominantly white men environments. Wrestling with all of the identities I carry and trying to hold on to my sense of self can be exhausting. Feeling like an impostor goes hand in hand with always feeling like an outsider.

As a leader, mentor, and executive coach, I've talked with hundreds of women. One of the most prevalent issues that arises is the sense of not being "good enough" or "being in over my head." One of the reasons I decided to write this book was to understand why so many successful women

---

259 Pauline Clance and Suzanne Imes, "The Imposter Phenomenon in High Achieving Women: Dynamics and Therapeutic Intervention," *Psychotherapy: Theory, Research & Practice* 15 no.3 (1978): 241–247.

suffer from feelings of inadequacy. My curiosity is more than an academic exercise; I have seen examples of impostor syndrome in my own life.

I remember standing on stage accepting an award, feeling unworthy, and wondering if they chose me by mistake. Just like so many other women of color, I have the added weight of feeling judged for being a Black woman. Jolie Doggett, writer and editor for *Medium*, wrote, "Imposter syndrome isn't just an imaginary voice in our heads. We can hear it loud and clear when we receive almost daily messages from society that we truly don't belong."[260]

## THE CONNECTION BETWEEN IMPOSTOR SYNDROME AND RACE

The concept of impostor syndrome has become a hot topic as America continues to grapple with racial and gender equality. While it's not exclusively an issue for women or women of color, we don't often hear successful men talk about feelings impostorism. In contrast, many successful women experience impostor syndrome, even at the height of their careers.

Valerie Young, a prominent lecturer on impostor syndrome and author of *The Secret Thoughts of Successful Women*, describes impostor syndrome as "always waiting for the other shoe to drop. You feel as if you've flown under the radar, been lucky or that they just like you. If you dismiss your accomplishments and abilities, you're left with one conclusion: That

---

260 Jolie Doggett, "Imposter Syndrome Hits Harder When You're Black," HuffPost, October 10, 2019, accessed September 12, 2020.

you've fooled them." Dr. Young says women in fields dominated by men are especially vulnerable to feeling like frauds because being an "other" breeds isolation and additional pressure to perform. In one study of engineering students, when the women watched a video featuring a large gender imbalance, their heart rates shot up. "It's stressful for women to walk into a room full of men," Young said.[261]

A study conducted by Kevin Cokley, a professor at the University of Texas at Austin, found that impostor syndrome can add to the stress minorities already feel. Dr. Cokley and his team of researchers collected surveys from 322 ethnic minority students—106 African Americans, 102 Asian Americans, and 108 Latinx Americans—on perceived discrimination, impostor feelings, and mental health. The study found that students in all ethnic minority groups reported similar levels of impostor feelings, although African American students reported more perceived discrimination. Dr. Cokley said, "Unlike white students who may experience impostorism, I believe that the ethnic minority student experience of impostorism is often racialized because ethnic minority students are aware of the stereotypes about intelligence that exist about their racial/ethnic groups."[262]

In an article in the *New York Times*, Dr. Cokley stated that although the study didn't definitively find that discrimination

---

261 Valerie Young, *The Secret Thoughts of Successful Women: Why Capable People Suffer from the Impostor Syndrome and How to Thrive in Spite of It* (New York: Crown Business, 2011).

262 Kevin Cokley et al, "Impostor Feelings as a Moderator and Mediator of the Relationship Between Perceived Discrimination and Mental Health Among Racial/Ethnic Minority College Students," *Journal of Counseling Psychology* vol. 64 no.2 (2017): 141-154.

causes impostorism, he believes there's a link between the two issues. He explained, "Feeling like an impostor can exacerbate the impact of discrimination. This is what we found with African American students in our study." Dr. Cokley admitted that he was inspired to study impostor syndrome because of his experiences as an African American scholar, researcher, and psychologist. "I felt like an impostor, I felt like people were looking at me and that I was going to be found out as not belonging there," he said.[263]

Men may experience self-doubt and lack of belonging in academia. However, being a woman and a person of color means being susceptible to experiences of racism and sexism that can amplify the likelihood of impostor phenomenon. The intersection of race and gender for women of color in academia is important because both identities can heavily impact women of color and their academic experience, especially if their identities are visible.[264]

Common causes of impostor syndrome include feelings such as stigma, stereotype threat, or an overall sense of intellectual phoniness. A woman of color attending a predominantly white institution is likely to worry that her accomplishments are not good enough relative to her peers' accomplishments. These thoughts could derive from feeling that she was accepted into a university because of affirmative action or by accident.[265]

---

263 Kristin Wong, "Dealing with Impostor Syndrome When You're Treated as an Impostor," *New York Times,* June 12, 2018.

264 Cokley et al, "Imposter Feelings."

265 Darlene Miller and Signe Kastberg, *"Of Blue Collars and Ivory Towers: Women from Blue-Collar Backgrounds in Higher Education,"* *Roeper Review* 18 no.1(September 1995): 27–33.

Dr. Cokley's researchers found that African American students with high impostor feelings were likely to feel anxiety and depression caused by the impact of perceived discrimination. In response to the microaggressions minorities experience in the external environment, thoughts and feelings turn into a negative internal dialogue that can result in poor physical and mental health. Impostor syndrome makes it easy to believe the lies from both society and our brain.[266]

Impostor syndrome lives in the minds of those who suffer from its effects.[267] There are no external cues that give away the struggles happening on the inside. Women at the highest levels of achievement still carry the scars. The only clue is in the stories they tell.

Impostor syndrome can affect women at any age, no matter their level of success. Tina Fey is a true renaissance woman—a comedian, best-selling author, director, and television and Broadway producer. Her motto, "fake it 'til you make it," has become so widespread that it's even easier to believe your accomplishments don't deserve the praise they get. In an interview, Tina Fey admitted, "The beauty of the impostor syndrome is you vacillate between extreme egomania, and a complete feeling of: 'I'm a fraud! Oh god, they're on to me! I'm a fraud!' So, you just try to ride the egomania when it comes and enjoy it, and then slide through the idea of fraud."[268]

---

266 Cokley et al, "Imposter Feelings."
267 Young, "Secret Thoughts of Successful Women."
268 Jane Burnett, "6 Powerful People on How They Manage Their Imposter Syndrome," Thrive Global, December 7, 2018, accessed July 15, 2020.

Even the most successful of us experience impostor syndrome. Civil rights activist, author, poet, and Nobel Laureate Dr. Maya Angelou admitted that she often felt like a fraud. She once said, "I have written 11 books, but each time I think, 'uh oh, they're going to find out now. I've run a game on everybody, and they're going to find me out.'" Former First Lady Michelle Obama said, "Imposter syndrome is so tough. We doubt our own judgment, our own abilities, and our own reasons for being where we are. Even when we know better, it can still lead to us playing it small and not standing in our full power."[269]

## YOU DON'T NEED PERMISSION TO TAKE YOUR SEAT AT THE TABLE

In the fall of 2018, I volunteered for the Library of Congress's National Book Festival, one of the largest gatherings in the country focused on reading and literacy. It's the book lover's equivalent to Comic-Con. There were hundreds of volunteers supporting the Library of Congress staff to handle a crowd of over two hundred thousand people. The main stage speaker that year was Supreme Court Justice and author Sonia Sotomayor. There were so many people wanting to see her that the vast hall quickly filled to capacity, and three thousand people had to be turned away.[270]

The audience of over one thousand rose to their feet and cheered as Justice Sotomayor strode confidently onto the

---

269 Jessica Bennett, "How to Overcome 'Impostor Syndrome'," *New York Times*, accessed March 18, 2020.

270 Ron Charles, "National Book Festival in Washington Breaks Attendance and Sales Records," *Washington Post*, September 3, 2018.

stage. She looked elegant and composed, wearing a vibrant green and white dress with a coordinating sweater. Justice Sotomayor exuded a quiet confidence, and you could see a sparkle in her eyes as she surveyed the crowd. She was warm and engaging as she told her rags-to-riches story.[271] I remember tears of pride welling in my eyes as Carla Hayden, the first woman and the first African American Librarian of Congress, interviewed Justice Sotomayor, the first Hispanic Supreme Court Justice.[272]

Despite being the first Hispanic person on the US Supreme Court, Justice Sonia Sotomayor admitted to feeling like a fraud and not fitting in throughout much of her life. She grew up in a Bronx housing project with her mother and brother. Justice Sotomayor remembered staying within a few blocks of her home, never straying far from her neighborhood. She said, "I explored the world through books. I saw the possibility of things I couldn't imagine without reading." She was diagnosed with diabetes at the age of seven but found the courage to deal with her disease through comic books. Imagining that she was a superhero filled her with the strength to brave daily insulin shots. Although comfortable in her neighborhood, Justice Sotomayor knew she would have to leave its safe confines once she graduated from high school.[273]

Justice Sotomayor had never thought of herself as a likely candidate for Princeton University before the school accepted

271  *Library of Congress*, "U.S. Supreme Court Justice Sonia Sotomayor: 2018 National Book Festival," October 18, 2018, video, 57:44.

272  "About the Librarian," Library of Congress, accessed March 28, 2020.

273  Sonia Sotomayor, "My Beloved World," (New York: Random House, 2013).

her application. She described her time at the university as a life-changing experience. When she arrived on campus, she said it was like "a visitor landing in an alien country." Justice Sotomayor battled anxiety and self-doubt at Princeton that followed her to Yale Law School and her legal career. She said, "I have spent my years since Princeton, while at law school and in my various professional jobs, not feeling completely a part of the worlds I inhabit. I am always looking over my shoulder wondering if I measure up."[274]

She confessed, "For a lot of my life I would be afraid, I would have self-doubt, and I would try to power through." When she was nominated for the Supreme Court, there were some who thought she wasn't smart enough to be on the high court. She felt hurt by their comments but refused to allow someone else's opinions to deter her. "Never let anyone tell you what you can't do and know that you can do anything!" Justice Sotomayor learned to deal with self-doubt and feelings of impostorism by sharing her feelings with other people. Her mantra is, "Together, all of us who are different create a better world."[275]

Recognition is another critical step in breaking the cycle of impostor syndrome. Dr. Valerie Young suggests allowing yourself the lenience to make mistakes and learn from them. She believes defining competence as the ability to figure something out rather than having all the answers. Accepting that you really do belong is important. She says, "Women

---

274  Ibid.
275  *Library of Congress,* "Justice Sotomayor."

keep waiting for permission to take a seat at the table. Let's stop waiting for permission."[276]

I still struggle with bouts of impostor syndrome, but knowing I'm not alone has helped me gain control over feeling like a fraud. I've realized that my imperfections, my struggles, and my story are what contribute to my greatness. I had to stop beating myself up for not being perfect and for thinking I had to pretend to be something other than who I am in order for people to accept me.

## YOUR IDENTITY IS YOUR SUPERPOWER

Actress and producer America Ferrera is breaking down barriers in Hollywood and opening doors as the first Latina actress to win an Emmy Award in a lead category. She creates multidimensional characters who empower girls and women to embrace their unique identities. Ferrera believes her identity isn't an obstacle. She once said that if she could go back and have a conversation with her nine-year-old self, she would tell her, "My identity is my superpower!"[277]

Ferrera believes that as women of color, our presence in the workplace creates possibilities. She refuses to internalize the negative stereotypes that our society has placed on women and people of color. She firmly believes that change will come when we question our fundamental values and beliefs.

276 Young, "Secret Thoughts of Successful Women."
277 TED, "My identity is a Superpower - Not an Obstacle | America Ferrera," June 21, 2019, video, 14:02.

Ferrera said, "Each of us must see to it that our actions lead to our best intentions."[278]

Showing up and owning your full identity matters. You never know whose life will be lifted by seeing someone who lets them know it's okay to be different and to speak up for yourself. Malala Yousafzai, the youngest person ever to win the Nobel Peace Prize, credits Ferrera with inspiring her to use her voice.[279] Malala was only eleven years old when she began writing blogs for BBC advocating education for girls and bringing attention to the oppression of the Taliban regime in her native Pakistan. At the age of fifteen, she survived an assassination attempt by a Taliban gunman who shot her in the head as she rode a bus home from school. Despite her grievous injury, Malala continued to speak out on issues of women's education and the plight of refugees.[280]

On July 12, 2013, Malala's sixteenth birthday, she gave her first public speech since the assassination attempt.[281] She said, "The terrorists thought they would change my aims and stop my ambitions, but nothing changed in my life except this: weakness, fear, and hopelessness died. Strength, power, and courage was born." In 2014, she was awarded the Nobel

278 Ibid.

279 *SuperPopVIP*, "America Ferrera Introduces Malala Yousafzai at Glamour Magazine's 23rd Annual Women of The Year Awards Event at the Carnegie Hall," November 24, 2013, video, 1:07.

280 "Malala's Story," Malala Fund, accessed March 28, 2020.

281 "Shot Pakistan Schoolgirl Malala Yousafzai Addresses UN," BBC News, July 12, 2014, accessed March 28, 2020.

Peace Prize, which had previously been given to her heroes Martin Luther King Jr. and Nelson Mandela.[282]

## KEY TAKEAWAYS

People with impostor syndrome incorrectly attribute their success to luck or interpret it as a result of deceiving others into thinking they're more intelligent than they perceive themselves to be. While early research focused on the prevalence of impostor syndrome among high-achieving women, it affects both men and women equally. However, women of color may bear additional burdens that come with racial stereotyping.

As a leader, I have a responsibility to create a work environment that allows everyone to bring their gifts and talents forward. I have to model the behaviors I want to see from others. In order to do that, I had to change the stories I told myself. Once I started to embrace a new narrative, I noticed that the voice inside my head that once provided a running commentary for my faults began to change. Today, I still get flashes of negativity, but I've learned to reframe the narrative toward positivity. Now the voice in my head belongs to me.

---

282 "The Nobel Peace Prize for 2014," The Nobel Prize, accessed March 28, 2020.

**CHAPTER 12**

# THE MAKING OF A LEADER

---

But little by little, / as you left their voices behind, / the stars began to burn / through the sheets of clouds, / and there was a new voice / which you slowly / recognized as your own, / that kept you company / as you strode deeper and deepe r/ into the world, / determined to do / the only thing you could do – / determined to save / the only life you could save.

–MARY OLIVER[283]

Mary Oliver's poem "The Journey" captures the essence of the reluctant hero's awakening.[284] The opening verse reads,

---

283 Mary Oliver, *Dream Work* (Boston: Atlantic Monthly Press, 1986).
284 Ibid.

"One day you finally knew / what you had to do and began / though the voices around you kept shouting their bad advice." We're all on a journey to find ourselves, our peace, and our place in this world. Some of us embark on heroic crusades like Don Quixote, while most of us are reluctant heroes just trying to get through the chaos of daily life.

"The Journey" reminds me of all the times in my life and career when I realized that it was time to take a different path. Those pivotal moments have pushed me to grow in ways that could only happen once I left my comfort zone.

## THE HERO'S JOURNEY

Joseph Campbell first defined the hero's journey, a myth-based framework of the traditional hero's adventure. Campbell was a professor of literature at Sarah Lawrence College whose work covered many aspects of the human experience. He was best-known for his book *The Hero with a Thousand Faces* that focused on his theory of the monomyth that explains the epic journey of the classic hero common in mythologies throughout the world.[285] In the seven decades since the publication of *The Hero with a Thousand Faces*, Campbell's theories have been used in literature and films to depict the journey of discovery.

Campbell also coined the phrase "follow your bliss" to describe his philosophical admonition for all of us to leave the ordinary world behind and set off in search of the

---

285 Joseph Campbell, *The Hero with a Thousand Faces* Campbell (Princeton, N.J.: Princeton University Press, 2004).

extraordinary. He derived this idea from ancient Sanskrit texts that described "the jumping-off place to the ocean of transcendence." He saw "follow your bliss" as a mantra and as a helpful guide for the hero's journey that each of us embarks on. He said, "If you follow your bliss, you put yourself on a kind of track that has been there all the while, waiting for you, and the life that you ought to be living is the one you are living. Wherever you are—if you are following your bliss, you are enjoying that refreshment, that life within you, all the time."[286]

Campbell's fingerprints can be seen in the work of famed Hollywood writer, director, and producer George Lucas, who has credited Campbell for influencing his *Star Wars* saga. Lucas created the *Star Wars* media franchise in 1977. His first film has expanded into many other films, television series, video games, novels, comic books, and theme park attractions.[287] The franchise holds a Guinness World Records title for the "Most successful film merchandising franchise." In 2020, the franchise's total value was estimated at over $70 billion, making it the fifth highest-grossing media franchise of all time.[288]

286 Joseph Campbell, "Joseph Campbell and the Power of Myth with Bill Moyers," edited by Betty Sue Flowers (New York: Doubleday and Co., 1988), 113.

287 "A Dummy's Guide to the Star Wars Universe for Those Who Feel the Force," *The Sunday Guardian,* March 10, 2016, accessed March 26, 2020.

288 "1977: Highest-Grossing Sci-F Series at the Box Office", Guinness World Records, August 19, 2015, accessed July 4, 2020.

## THE CRUCIBLE

I have an affinity for turtles. I'm not talking about your average little pet store variety. I mean the big, slow-moving turtles I saw growing up in Florida. The fable about the tortoise and the hare always resonated with me because the underdog ultimately won the day. The tortoise is the strategic thinker that uses its intellect to outsmart the fast-moving hare. My hero in victory is usually the unassuming underdog that comes through to save the day.

The turtle withdraws into its shell at the first sign of conflict. My aversion to conflict goes back to childhood. I was raised in a family that didn't show strong emotions. We were never overly affectionate, and I never saw my parents argue.

As an extremely shy and introverted kid, I hated going to school. I was uncomfortable around people and my mother literally had to drag me out of the car every morning. It was the same routine every morning for almost a year.

When I entered the workforce, I was comfortable being a team player, never speaking up, and never standing out. I was quiet, introverted, and socially awkward. I enjoyed figuring out how things worked and then how to streamline and improve the process. My ideal job was working by myself in a quiet office, never needing to interact with others.

My quiet, ordered existence changed the night I survived Hurricane Andrew tearing through southern Florida.

This watershed moment happened on August 24, 1992. For the first time in my life, death was an imminent, possible option.

The night before, I drew the short straw and had to work a midnight shift at the FAA's Miami International Flight Service Station. I was a new supervisor and my job was to help get as many small airplanes out of the line of the storm as we could before the weather forced us to shut down the airport.

The local National Weather Service office had assured us that we were outside of the evacuation zone. The facility had a generator, a full refrigerator, and long-range weather radar. A number of the staff brought their families and pets of every variety to ride out the storm.

Shortly after midnight, the hurricane shutters gave way and the roof began to peel away. It felt like the longest night of my life. I wasn't a particularly religious person, but I prayed that God would help us to survive. "Please, Lord hold this building together!" Even our resident atheist, who was cowering under the sink in the women's restroom, joined in the prayer circle, adding strength to our pleas. He repeated over and over, "God, if you exist, I promise to believe if You let me live through this!"

Once the wind subsided, we walked out in the early morning light to a sea of destruction comparable to an old disaster movie. Airplanes were wrapped around telephone poles, trees were pulled up by their roots, and cars were damaged beyond recognition.

Something changed in me after that night. I emerged with a sense of gratitude and an appreciation for life. I think I lost my fears of failure, rejection, and not being good enough.

I learned how to trust God and how to trust myself. I stopped waiting for life to change and started moving forward. I took baby steps at first, like getting out of South Florida. I eventually became more open and freer. This freedom to let people in has changed the way I engage with my family, colleagues, and most importantly, the people I lead.

## CRUCIBLE LEADERSHIP

Warren Bennis, dubbed the "dean of leadership gurus" by the *Forbes Magazine*, believed that leadership was a personal journey of self-discovery.[289] He said that "leaders are made not born" and are formed out of crucible moments that prepare them to lead. As he wrote in *On Becoming a Leader*, "Before people can learn to lead, they must learn something about this strange new world."[290]

Bennis, through his decades of studying leadership, explored how the crucible experience is instrumental in shaping leadership qualities. He said, "We found that something magical happens in the crucible—an alchemy whereby fears, and suffering are transformed into something glorious and redemptive."[291] He believed that crucible experiences reveal instead of create leaders. The process of experiencing the crucible unlocks the leader within us and showcases the leader's ability to inspire others.

---

289 Jena McGregor, "Remembering Leadership Sage Warren Bennis," *Washington Post*, August 4, 2014, On Leadership.

290 Warren Bennis, *On Becoming a Leader* (New York: Basic Books, 2009).

291 Ibid.

Bennis and Robert Thomas led the *Harvard Business Review* study "Crucibles of Leadership." They wrote, "A crucible is, by definition, a transformative experience through which an individual comes to a new or an altered sense of identity." The authors of the study went on to describe the crucible experience as a test or trial that forces leaders to reflect on and reevaluate who they are and what matters to them. They said that crucible moments "required them to examine their values, question their assumptions and hone their judgment."[292]

According to "Crucibles of Leadership," one of the most common types of crucibles involves the experience of prejudice.[293] I can speak from personal experience that being subjected to prejudice and bigotry can be traumatizing. Being called the N-word on more than one occasion is like being punched in the gut. As Bennis and Thomas wrote, "Being a victim of prejudice is particularly traumatic because it forces an individual to confront a distorted picture of him or herself, and it often unleashes profound feelings of anger, bewilderment, and even withdrawal." They found that the experience of prejudice can also serve as a wakeup call to the victim. They wrote, "Through it, they gain a clearer vision of who they are, the role they play, and their place in the world."[294]

Bennis and Thomas believe that great leaders possess four essential skills, and those same skills allow us to find meaning in our crucible moments. The four skills are

---

292 Warren Bennis, and Robert Thomas, "Crucibles of Leadership," *Harvard Business Review 80 no. 124 (September 2002): 39-45.*
293 Ibid.
294 Ibid.

- The ability to engage others in shared meaning
- A distinctive and compelling voice
- A sense of integrity and strong set of values
- "Adaptive capacity" or applied creativity

They ranked this final skill as the most important, calling it "an almost magical ability to transcend adversity, with all its attendant stresses, and to emerge stronger than before."[295]

In an interview, Warren Bennis once said, "The thing about leadership is realizing something about your capacities, your agency. You are really the author of your own life. No one else is going to do it for you." Bennis also said a combination of hardiness and the ability to grasp context allows leaders to persevere, gain strength, and emerge from the crucible more engaged and committed than before. Hardiness is the perseverance and toughness that enable people to emerge from devastating circumstances without losing hope. He explained, "These attributes allow leaders to grow from their crucibles, instead of being destroyed by them—to find opportunity where others might find only despair. This is the stuff of true leadership."[296]

## KEY TAKEAWAYS
Leaders are made, not born. They start with their unique identity shaped by experience, hardships, relationships, and courage. Each of us is like a diamond. We start out rough, unshaped, and undeveloped. Life is the master stonecutter.

---

295 Ibid.
296 Ibid.

Our crucible moments serve to cut away the excess stone and shape the person we are today. Our own individual hero's journey reveals the many facets of our identity that make us unique. Great leaders draw strength from the crucibles they experience on the journey.

Hero's journeys and crucible moments are transformative points in the making of great leaders. Each of us will be tested, and some of us will face many pivotal junctures that will push us to the limits of our capacity. Noted author, pastor, and gospel singer Wintley Phipps said, "It is in the quiet crucible of your personal, private sufferings that your noblest dreams are born, and God's greatest gifts are given."[297] Just know that you have the strength to not just survive, but to come through stronger than before.

Bennis believed that leaders who always see the silver lining even in the worst situations, possess a trait he called hardiness, a term he borrowed from positive psychology.[298] He likened hardiness to resilience and the ability to focus on the future. He said, "I think every great leader without exception has that resilience, that positive outlook—the 'nothing to fear but fear itself,' the 'we shall overcome someday.'"[299]

In hindsight, my crucible moments have led to the greatest opportunities for me. The lessons I learned during and after the hurricane set me on the path to finding my voice. They sent me on other journeys that led to other crucibles. Each

---

297 "Wintley Phipps Quotes," Goodreads, accessed March 28, 2020.
298 Bennis and Thomas, "Crucibles of Leadership."
299 Ibid.

experience, though difficult, ultimately made me a stronger person and a better leader. A Maya Angelou quote hangs on the wall in my office and inspires me to keep going on and to enjoy the journey: "My mission in life is not merely to survive, but to thrive; and to do so with some passion, some compassion, some humor, and some style."[300] Passion, compassion, humor, style, and—I'll add my personal favorite—grace, are the perfect ingredients for great leadership.

---

300 "Maya Angelou: In Her Own Words," US and Canada, BBC News, May 28, 2014, accessed March 28, 2020.

# CHAPTER 13

# AUTHENTIC LEADERSHIP

———

To be authentic is the highest form of praise.
You're fulfilling your mission and purpose on
earth when you honor the real you.

—OPRAH WINFREY[301]


I consider myself an odd duck because I've never found anyone who thinks like me or acts like me. I was a shy, introverted kid who loved books, music, and television. My siblings hated my taste in books (anything by Stephen King), music (pop), and television (sci-fi or Westerns). To my Southern household, my refusal to eat eggs or grits was sacrilegious. As you can see, I've always charted my own path. It can be lonely at times, but I'm happy being authentically me. Paulo Coelho, the Brazilian author who has sold over 175 million books, speaks eloquently of the solitary nature of discovering

———

301 Oprah Winfrey, "What Oprah Knows for Sure About Authenticity," *Oprah.com*, accessed Mar 28, 2020.

your true self. Coelho said, "Some people around you will not understand your journey. They don't need to, it's not for them."[302]

Creating an authentic life is like an artist creating a work of art. Sarah Ban Breathnach wrote in her book *Simple Abundance: A Daybook of Comfort and Joy,* "With every choice, every day, you are creating a unique work of art. [...] Each time you experience the new, you become receptive to inspiration."[303] The art of authentic leadership starts with finding out who you are and using that knowledge to connect with others.

I wanted to find people who have mastered the art of authenticity. That search led me to Caroline McHugh.

## ONE TRUE NOTE

On a beautiful spring afternoon, I received text message from a friend that included a link to a YouTube video. Accompanying the video link was a cryptic note that read, "Just watch, you'll understand!" My first thought was that this must be some kind of scam or her account had been hacked. I called her to confirm that the message was legitimate. She said, "Yes, I sent it. Just watch it and we can talk after." Now I was really curious. I had to see what had gotten my normally stoic friend so excited.

302 Paulo Coelho, @paulocoelho, January 20, 2019, accessed March 28, 2020.

303 Sarah Ban Breathnach, *Simple Abundance: A Daybook of Comfort and Joy* (New York: Warner Books, 1995).

As I opened the link, I thought it might be an episode of Star Trek.[304] However, it was a TED Talk called "The art of being yourself."[305] It began with a tall, slender woman striding across the stage wearing a black robe that reminded me of something a Buddhist monk might wear. Her closely cropped hair made me think of an alien priestess. She began to speak in a thick Scottish brogue that possessed the rapturous cadence of a seasoned storyteller. This TED Talk with almost 9 million views was my introduction to Caroline McHugh, or "baby buddha," as she calls herself.[306]

Caroline McHugh is an entrepreneur, teacher, coach, and author committed to helping business leaders embrace the idea of being authentic versions of themselves. She delivers keynotes and masterclasses at dozens of Fortune 500 companies on engaging authenticity in leadership and in life. She wrote about her unique perspectives in her book, *Never Not a Lovely Moon: The Art of Being Yourself.*[307]

"We all have one true note we were destined to sing. When you figure out how to be yourself it's an incredibly liberating, untragic way to go through life." That statement from Caroline McHugh hit home for me. The search for my "one true note" has been the goal of my personal hero's journey. I believe we're all on that journey to find our authentic selves. As she put it, "When it comes to being yourself, needing other people's approval, loving somebody else's opinion, and

---

304  "Star Trek: The Original Series," IMDb, accessed September 22, 2020.

305  *TEDxTalks*, "The Art of Being Yourself," video, February 15, 2013, 26:23.

306  Ibid.

307  Caroline McHugh, *Never Not a Lovely Moon: The Art of Being Yourself* (Wilmington, OH: Orange Frazer Press, 2009).

mistaking it for your own is one of the most debilitating things you'll do on the road to being yourself."[308]

Another one of the worst things you can do on the road to finding your authentic self is to think small and play it safe for fear of drawing attention to yourself. Caroline wisely points out that most people live their lives not taking up enough of the space they're destined to hold. She says, "We take up this wee space around our toes." She added that when we see someone living life to the fullest, they can appear larger than life. "They're at least a foot bigger in every direction than normal human beings, and they shine, they gleam, they glow. It's like they've swallowed the moon."[309]

Caroline McHugh describes her job as "helping people find more and more ways of combining who they are with what they do."[310] This is a perfect example of the work of a leader: helping others harness their unique talents and abilities in service of the organization's mission. The important thing to remember is that each person's gifts are uniquely their own. Just like snowflakes and butterflies, no two are exactly alike. Philosopher and poet Ralph Waldo Emerson wrote, "No matter what your work, let it be your own. No matter what your occupation, let what you are doing be organic. Let it be in your bones. In this way, you will open the door by which the affluence of heaven and earth shall stream into you."[311]

---

308 *TEDxTalks*, "The Art of Being Yourself."

309 Ibid.

310 Ibid.

311 "Ralph Waldo Emerson," AZQuotes, accessed September 13, 2020.

Researchers are exploring the implications of authenticity in the workplace. One study found that the more authentic employees feel, the greater their job satisfaction, engagement, and self-reported performance.[312] Researcher Vanessa Buote wrote an article for the *Harvard Business Review* highlighting that it takes time for people to feel comfortable bringing their authenticity into the workplace. She found that "most people actively manage behavior, emotions, or the way we are perceived by coworkers and bosses for a variety of reasons."[313] For example, some employees don't feel free to express emotion or their sense of humor at work. "Others feel they must 'have it all together' or risk hurting their reputation or credibility." Buote's research revealed that 72 percent of people said it took an average of two to three months to show their true selves, with 60 percent of that group needing three months. The study also found that 22 percent of employees needed up to nine months to feel comfortable and authentically themselves, 9 percent needed between ten and twelve months, and another 9 percent reported that it took more than one year to show their true selves.[314]

Judy Murray, sports coach and mother of Wimbledon tennis champion Andy Murray, told a reporter for the *Guardian* how Caroline McHugh changed the course of her life. During the 2012 Olympics in London, Murray attended a female coaching workshop where Caroline McHugh was the closing

---

312   Ralph van den Bosch and Toon Taris, "Authenticity at Work: Development and Validation of an Individual Authenticity Measure at Work," *Journal of Happiness* 15 no. 1 (January 2014).

313   Vanessa Buote, "Most Employees Feel Authentic at Work, but It Can Take a While," *Harvard Business Review* (May 11, 2016).

314   Ibid.

speaker. She said McHugh's words left her "gobsmacked." The two women spoke after the speech and McHugh told Murray that each of us must "star in the movie of our life." She also told Murray, "You have a voice and you should use it." That encouragement gave Murray the push she needed to step out of her comfort zone and, as she said, "I'm not sure I have shut up since."[315]

Murray specifically credits McHugh with inspiring her to speak up and share her coaching philosophy. That pivotal meeting truly changed Judy Murray from an insecure woman into a role model for women coaches and an advocate for women's sport. Murray subsequently became an Officer of the Most Excellent Order of the British Empire (OBE), a recognition given to roughly five hundred people each year who have made big impacts in business, media, or charity.[316]

According to Caroline McHugh, all the work she's done has led her to the belief that individuality really is all it's cracked up to be. She professes that people who are afraid to be authentic are attracted to those who have the confidence to be themselves. "People who are frightened to be themselves will work for those who aren't afraid."[317]

### THE HALLMARKS OF AUTHENTIC LEADERSHIP

In 2015, Herminia Ibarra declared in *Harvard Business Review*, "Authenticity has emerged as the gold standard for

---

315  Judy Murray, "A New Start: Judy Murray on the 'Baby Buddhist' Who Cured Her Terror of Public Speaking," *The Guardian*, January 31, 2018.
316  Ibid.
317  *TEDxTalks*, "The Art of Being Yourself."

leadership."[318] Authentic leadership is defined as a pattern of behavior that promotes a positive ethical climate, fosters greater self-awareness, contains an internalized moral perspective, and encourages transparency.[319] The major themes that emerge from a review of the authentic leadership literature are a focus on self-awareness, an emphasis on the true self, and a grounding in moral leadership. An important distinction between authentic leadership and other theories of leadership is the prominence of the deep sense of self on the part of the leader.[320]

In 2003 Bill George was the CEO of Medtronic, the multi-billion-dollar Fortune 500 medical device company, when he co-wrote the book *Authentic Leadership: Rediscovering the Secrets to Creating Lasting Value*. He and his research team proposed a new kind of leader for whom character mattered more than characteristics or style. He drew from over thirty years of experience in the business world to develop his theory on the five dimensions of leadership.[321] The five dimensions are

1. Passion
2. Values

318  Herminia Ibarra, "The Authenticity Paradox," *Harvard Business Review* (January - February 2015).

319  Fred Walumbwa et al, "Authentic Leadership: Development and Validation of a Theory-Based Measure," *Journal of Management* 34 no. 1 (February 2008): 89–126.

320  Bruce Avolio and William Gardner, "Authentic Leadership Development: Getting to the Root of Positive Forms of Leadership," *The Leadership Quarterly* 16 no. 3 (May 2005): 315-338.

321  Bill George et al, "Discovering Your Authentic Leadership," *Harvard Business Review* (February 2007).

3. Relationships
4. Self-discipline
5. Heart

George wrote the characteristics of authentic leaders who embody the five dimensions: understanding their purpose, practicing solid values, establishing connected relationships, demonstrating self-discipline, and leading with heart. George believes leaders are not born with these characteristics, but they develop them over the course of a lifetime. He and his team challenged older models of leadership such as the "Great Man Theory." They noted that previous generations focused on "marketing" themselves as leaders rather than undertaking the deep transformational work of development.[322]

## AUTHENTICITY LOOKS DIFFERENT FOR WOMEN AND PEOPLE OF COLOR

According to a 2015 research study, "Authentic Leadership: Application to Women Leaders," men-oriented definitions of authenticity may be problematic for women and people of color. The researchers found there's frequently a "double-bind dilemma" that forces women to make a choice between displaying traditionally feminine behaviors or men-oriented standards of leadership behaviors. They also reported that organizations with men-oriented cultures require women to fit into men-dominated environments. Being true to yourself is even more difficult if you have a more feminine perspective of the self in relation to others. The report recommends that

322 Ibid.

the concept of authentic leadership expand to encompass a gender-neutral construct.[323]

Anka Wittenberg, senior vice president and chief diversity and inclusion officer at SAP Software Solutions, confirms that the corporate world enforces a masculine model for leadership. Women have been advised to use masculine body language, lower their natural speaking voices, and avoid feminine attire in order to be taken seriously. She also notes that many LGBTQ people in leadership positions believe they must mask their sexual orientation to be viewed as an effective leader.[324]

Leaders who feel they must hide important aspects of their identity find it hard to relax at work and spend considerable energy covering up their differences in an attempt to fit in. By compromising their identities, leaders tend to be less productive and to experience higher rates of burnout. Some researchers believe that inauthentic employees may be as much as 20 percent less productive than those who feel comfortable presenting their authentic identities to the world.[325]

As a woman of color, I have found that the combination of my gender and skin color does not fit the model of mainstream leadership. *Fortune* writer Ellen McGirt calls Black women

---

323  Margaret Hopkins and Deborah O'Neil, "Authentic Leadership: Application to Women Leaders," *Frontiers in Psychology* 6 no. 959 (July 15, 2015).

324  Anka Wittenberg, "The Business Impact of Authentic Leadership," *Entrepreneur*, April 20, 2015.

325  Ibid.

"double outsiders" because we aren't white or men.[326] I can only apply the mantra of "be yourself" only in spaces where I feel psychologically safe. There are times when I'm guarded for my own protection. Diahann Billings-Burford, CEO of Ross Initiative in Sports for Equality (RISE), wisely noted, "Authenticity when you are part of the "others" is a challenge, especially when you are leading groups that involve the mainstream."[327]

Many of us use mechanisms to protect ourselves. Psychologist Rick Hanson explained, "Most of us wear a kind of mask, a persona that hides our deepest thoughts and feelings, and presents a polished, controlled face to the world."[328] I learned to let go of the mask by getting a clear understanding of who I am and what matters most and by focusing on my core values. Diahann Billings-Burford says, "If you are 'other' in any way, your self-definition has to be constant." She elaborated, "You must maintain integrity about who you are and who you're going to be, no matter what situation you're in."[329]

Ann Fudge is the former chairman and CEO of Young & Rubicam and a member of the board of directors of General Electric, Novartis, Unilever, and Infosys. She was also inducted into the American Academy of Arts and Sciences in 2019 and is one of only a handful of African American

---

326 Ellen McGirt, "The Black Ceiling: Why African-American Women Aren't Making It to the Top in Corporate America, *Fortune Magazine*, September 27, 2017, accessed September 13, 2020.

327 *NYU Leads*, "Authentic Leadership as a Woman of Color," May 6, 2016, video, 5:59.

328 *Rick Hanson, "Who Is Behind the Mask?", Your Wise Brain(blog), Psychology Today, March 17, 2011.*

329 *NYU Leads*, "Authentic Leadership."

women to have led a Fortune 500 company.[330] She was one of 125 leaders that Bill George and his team interviewed for the book *Authentic Leadership*. Ann Fudge believes that anyone at any level in an organization can lead authentically. She said, "All of us have the spark of leadership in us, whether it is in business, in government, or as a nonprofit volunteer. The challenge is to understand ourselves well enough to discover where we can use our leadership gifts to serve others."[331]

Bronnie Ware worked in end-of-life care, capturing the biggest regrets of her clients. She compiled them into a book: *The Top Five Regrets of the Dying: A Life Transformed by the Dearly Departing.* She observed that the number one regret almost every one of her dying patients had was "I wish I'd had the courage to live a life true to myself, not the life others expected of me."[332]

## KEY TAKEAWAYS

I learned a valuable lesson by watching Caroline McHugh's video: "We all have one true note we were destined to sing."[333] Being authentic means living my life out loud. Allowing the me who exists on the inside to come to the surface has been liberating, like a butterfly emerging from its cocoon. My desire now is to find others of my tribe and serve as a guide to those who are still on the journey.

---

330 "Ann Fudge," The HistoryMakers, accessed September 22, 2020.

331 George et al, "Discovering Your Authentic Leadership."

332 Bronnie Ware, *The Top Five Regrets of the Dying: A Life Transformed by the Dearly Departing* (Carlsbad, CA: Hay House, 2012).

333 *TEDxTalks*, "The Art of Being Yourself."

Being inauthentic is exhausting! Pretending to be a certain way to fit in erodes confidence. What does authenticity look like for you? The answer to that question can unlock your greatness. Self-confidence is built on the foundation of authenticity. When you're a "double outsider," you better know who you are.

Too many of us are caught in the trap of trying to be someone else. Herminia Ibarra said, "The only way we grow as leaders is by stretching the limits of who we are—doing new things that make us uncomfortable but that teach us through direct experience who we want to become."[334]

Feel good about how you're showing up in the world. Stand up for yourself and stop asking permission to be who you were meant to be. Be your own advocate!

---

334 Ibarra, "The Authenticity Paradox."

# CHAPTER 14

# THE THREE C'S OF LEADERSHIP

———

*Leadership is the art of accomplishing more than the science of management says is possible.*

–COLIN POWELL[335]

My leadership philosophy is based on three pillars: confidence, compassion, and character. Confidence comes from knowing who you are, owning your identity, and having the courage to be vulnerable. Compassion is caring enough to walk in someone else's shoes and being able to move from empathy to action. Character is living based on your core values and operating with integrity.

———

335  Oren Harari and Ryan Chris, *The Leadership Secrets of Colin Powell* (New York: McGraw-Hill/TDM Audio, 2003).

As an executive coach, I support my clients as they navigate the challenges of leadership. My coaching philosophy is focused on self-awareness, learning, growth, and discovery. Honesty, integrity, compassion, and humor help me connect with my clients. Every client is innately capable of achieving their goals. My role as a coach is to support them on their leadership journeys.

My job as a leader and as a coach is to facilitate their transformation by providing a safe, open, nonjudgmental environment while challenging them to be open to new possibilities. I believe in the greatness that lies within each of us and I'm committed to supporting leaders as they build the capacity to lead effectively in challenging times. To have lasting results, leaders must develop solutions and strategies that work for them both now and in the future. Reflection, practice, and accountability are foundational to sustained growth.

## THE RULES

A few years ago, I was sitting in my office avoiding the thing I hate most about being a leader: annual performance reviews. Don't get me wrong, I love helping others to grow and achieve greatness. I can shower praise as well as I can deliver tough critiques. However, I think performance management should be a part of the daily interactions with your team; I have never seen the value of waiting until the end of the year to talk with someone about their performance. It's either too late to allow for course corrections or not timely enough to recognize great performance. Anyway, I was procrastinating about completing the dreaded annual paperwork exercise when I started thinking back to the lessons I'd learned as a leader. There are some fundamental habits that have consistently helped me on my journey. These are the habits or rules as I see them:

### RULE 1: NO PITY PARTIES.

Feeling sorry for yourself can be a coping mechanism. It's a form of compassion we show ourselves. However, self-compassion can lead to self-pity and depression. Pastor and best-selling author Joyce Meyer said, "Self-pity is the most miserable party to go to, because, in case you haven't noticed, you're the only one who is there."[336] I usually give myself twenty-four hours to get over the self-pity I feel about the obstacle I'm facing, whatever it is and however hard it may be. Wallow in it, cry about it, get mad—whatever. Then, when your twenty-four hours are up, get up and figure out what you want to do from there. That's it. After that, it's time to get moving.

### RULE 2: LOOK OUT FOR YOUR TRIBE.

Seth Godin, entrepreneur and best-selling business writer, believes a tribe is "any group of people, large or small, who are connected to one another, a leader, and an idea." He goes on to say that shared interests and a common way to communicate differentiates a tribe from just a group of random individuals.[337] My second rule states that you must always look out for your tribe. Your tribe is your family, your circle,

---

336 Daniel Whyte III, *Letters to Young Black Women* (Torch Legacy Publications, 2006), 203.

337 Seth Godin, *Tribes: We Need You to Lead Us* (New York: Penguin Group, 2008).

the folks who work with and for you. You don't give them up to get ahead and don't ever forget that you need them more than they need you. Show love, appreciation, and gratitude. Kick butt and be ferociously honest when you need to. They're your tribe and your loyalty is to them. Help them focus on the prize, see the big picture, give them the tools they need, and get out of their way.

### RULE 3: TAKE CARE OF YOURSELF.

Self-care is a fundamental imperative of effective leadership. Anyone who has ever flown on a commercial aircraft has heard the instructions: "In the event that oxygen is needed, place the oxygen mask on yourself first." You cannot help anyone else if you burn yourself out. My third rule is take care of yourself mentally, physically, and spiritually. Health in all of those areas is required for you to do the work God put you here to do. He has blessed you with unique talents and abilities so you can live out your purpose. Executive coach and author Amy Jen Su said, "Self-care means that you're attuned to and understand what you need to be your most constructive, effective, and authentic self."[338] She insists that self-care is not optional. It must be integrated in a leader's daily routine.

### RULE 4: BE GRATEFUL.

Always, always, always be grateful for where you came from, what you went through, and the ability to stand where you

---

338 Amy Jen Su, *The Leader You Want to Be: Five Essential Principles for Bringing Out Your Best Self--Every Day* (Boston, MA: Harvard Business Review Press, 2019).

stand. No matter how hard your struggle has been, it's made you into the person you are today. My fourth rule is to be grateful for what you have been given. Alice Walker, author of *The Color Purple* said, "Thank You is the best prayer that anyone could say. I say that one a lot. Thank you expresses extreme gratitude, humility, understanding."[339] Recent research suggests that gratitude acts as a predictor of well-being and leads to lower levels of stress and depression over time.[340]

Gratitude also has a significant impact on business results. Chester Elton and Adrian Gostick conducted a 200,000-person study that found "managers that exhibit a high degree of gratitude lead teams with higher overall business results, including up to two times greater profitability than their peers, an average 20% higher customer satisfaction and significantly higher scores in employee engagement, including vital metrics such as trust and accountability."[341]

### RULE 5: SHARE YOUR TESTIMONY.

Leaders who know how to reflect on their life experiences in order to identify stories that shaped them are better able

---

339 "Alice Walker Quotes," BrainyQuote.com, accessed September 14, 2020.

340 Alex Wood, Stephen Joseph and John Maltby, "Gratitude Uniquely Predicts Satisfaction with Life: Incremental Validity Above the Domains and Facets of the Five Factor Model," *Personality and Individual Differences* 45 no. 1 (2008): 49-54.

341 Adrian Gostick and Chester Elton, *Leading with Gratitude: Eight Leadership Practices for Extraordinary Business Results*, (New York: Harper Business, 2020).

to communicate authentically with others.[342] My fifth rule requires us to know when and how to reveal our journey through stories. Share some of your struggles so that people who feel like they can't make it will see you as a light and be able to hold on for just another day. We need to understand that we don't have to be perfect to be great. Understand that perfection is a journey, not a destination.

**RULE 6: TRUST YOURSELF.**

Trust your gut, your heart, whatever that Spidey sense is telling you.[343] Trust yourself to know what opportunities to take and which ones to pass up. My sixth rule means trusting yourself to know when it's time for you to move from your comfy couch, your comfy job, or your comfy circle to the thing you're meant to do. Iyanla Vanzant, author, television personality, and motivational speaker, once said, "As you learn to TRUST YOURSELF something miraculous happens. You begin to TRUST THE PROCESS you are living and the miracles life brings!"[344] As a leader, your team will only trust you as much as you trust yourself. Trust is an act of vulnerability and courage that gets easier the more times you take that leap of faith.

---

342  Tommi Auvinen et al, "Evolution of Strategy Narration and Leadership Work in the Digital Era," *Leadership* 15 no. 2 (April 2019): 205–25.

343  Zac Zemantic, "Experiencing Spidey-Sense in Spider-Man: The Science Behind Science Fiction," *Down to a Science* (blog), *Connecticut Science Center*, accessed September 22, 2020.

344  Iyanla Vanzant @iyanlavanzant, "As you learn to TRUST YOURSELF," Twitter, September 1, 2013, 10:00 p.m.

## WHAT IS YOUR LEGACY?

*Life's most persistent and urgent question is, "What are you doing for others"*

−MARTIN LUTHER KING JR.[345]

Adhering to these rules will help you build the foundation for your legacy. Merriam-Webster's Dictionary defines legacy as "something transmitted by or received from an ancestor or predecessor or from the past."[346] How we're remembered is a function of how we live our lives and the impact we have on the world. Entrepreneur and motivational speaker Jim Rohn once said, "All good men and women must take responsibility to create legacies that will take the next generation to a level we could only imagine."[347]

My legacy is a compilation of my family's history and my story. Who I am and how I will be remembered is a work in progress. The journey to my legacy started as a lowly payroll clerk and turned into a senior executive running a $500 million enterprise.

I am a by-product of my grandparents who passionately supported their families with very little education but with phenomenal work ethic. In fact, my grandfather left school at the age of twelve to support his mother and younger sisters.

---

345 Martin Luther King, *Strength to Love* (New York: Harper & Row, 1963) 72.

346 *Merriam-Webster.com Dictionary*, s.v. "Legacy," accessed September 14, 2020.

347 Lydia Sweatt, "11 Quotes About Leaving a Legacy," *Success* (blog), accessed May 28, 2020.

My maternal grandmother didn't finish high school, but due to her keen business sense and commitment to customer service, she owned a restaurant for nearly fifty years. They passed their drive onto my parents, who were both the first in their families to attend college. From my family, I learned important values that serve me well to this day: the value of hard work (no task is ever too small, no matter your title), the importance of education (never stop learning), and most importantly, how to live life to the fullest (with family, friends, laughter, and faith).

Let's talk about your legacy. For some of you who are at the beginning of your leadership journey, this may seem like a topic for another year or, for some, another decade. However, your legacy isn't a distant milepost: you're writing the ending of your story today.

Ultimately, you'll be remembered for two things: how you show up on your worst days and how you show up on your best days. For me, the worst had to be the night of Hurricane Andrew when I was responsible for nineteen other people and twenty-seven animals as overnight watch supervisor. Everyone survived even though the building didn't. That night I learned a valuable lesson: take care of your team, create order from chaos as people look to you for direction, and have the courage to speak up for yourself and for others. My worst day as a leader turned out to be a pivotal point in my career.

One of the best days was November 2, 2017—the day of my retirement party—because I truly felt the impact of my thirty-four years of government service. I thought about the people I'd helped on the journey and the ones who had helped me. The best part of it was sharing the moment with my husband, my parents who are in their eighties now and with my big sister who couldn't resist telling embarrassing stories from our childhood.

We remember Abraham Lincoln for his leadership during one of the most chaotic and challenging times in our nation's history. His legacy is a reflection of how he handled adversity. He met incivility with kindness, panic with calm, territorialism with generosity, fear with faith, anger with love, anxiety with peace, and uncertainty with stability. A question that each leader has to answer is, "How will we handle our time in the crucible?"

Your legacy is who you are as a leader. You'll be remembered for your vision, your values, your ability to bring the best out in others, and engagement with your team.[348] The question isn't, "How engaged are your employees?" but rather, "How engaged are you? Are you fully present or just waiting for the next promotion?"

Be grateful for the gift of leadership. As a leader, you have the ability to fundamentally improve the lives of the people you lead. Don't take it for granted.

Your legacy will be defined by the times that you raise your hand, step forward when you would rather remain silent, and make the risky decision to say yes—yes to the unknown and to new possibilities. H. Jackson Brown Jr. (although it was

---

348 Aaron Brown, "How to Measure Employee Engagement the Right Way," Quantum Workplace, January 21, 2020, accessed September 14, 2020.

later attributed to Mark Twain) said, "Twenty years from now you will be more disappointed by the things you didn't do than by the ones you did do. So, throw off the bowlines. Sail away from the safe harbor. Catch the trade winds in your sails. Explore. Dream. Discover."[349]

Spend some time thinking about your legacy after finishing this book. What are you proud of? What should you do differently? Who are the people that helped shape you and your career? I would also invite you to open your hearts and minds to the possibility of writing a different ending to your story. Begin with the end in mind.[350]

The challenges presented by chaotic times can be daunting, but we all must move beyond fear and focus on solutions. As leaders, we should be the calm voice of reason that cuts through the turmoil. Great leaders exist for such a time and each of you has the capacity for greatness.

Albert Schweitzer was a renowned medical missionary, theologian, and organist who consistently raised money for hospitals in Africa. Schweitzer and his wife were French citizens at the outbreak of World War I. They refused to leave their beloved hospital in Lambaréné in French Equatorial Africa and ended up in a German internment camp. After the war, they resumed their lifesaving work, focusing on helping victims of leprosy. Schweitzer received the 1952 Nobel Peace

---

349  Quote Investigator, "Twenty Years From Now You Will Be More Disappointed By The Things You Didn't Do Than By The Ones You Did Do," September 29, 2011, accessed September 14, 2020.

350  Stephen Covey, *The 7 Habits Of Highly Effective People: Restoring The Character Ethic* (New York: Free Press, 2004).

Prize for his dedicated service to others.[351] He believed, "At times our own light goes out and is rekindled by a spark from another person. Each of us has cause to think with deep gratitude of those who have lighted the flame within us."[352] Each of us has the potential for being a beacon of light in challenging times.


## KEY TAKEAWAYS

The art of great leadership starts and ends with the heart. The heart unites, inspires, encourages, and cares. Once joined with the head, the body—an organization—thrives. Leading with the heart risks exposing your true self, unvarnished and vulnerable. Connection requires courage. You run the risk of being exposed, subjected to scrutiny, and being less than—less than perfect, not as smart, not as pretty. Resist the attack of the "nots." Exposure invites trust, connection, and love. Try to embrace the "I cans" and the "I ams."

There is power in the pivot. Energy is generated and released as we move from what was to what will be. Intention draws the picture and sets the course. The point of transition is where we're most vulnerable—we leave the security and protection of what we know. We shed the protective cover of the expert and we are left in the naked state of the novice. In order to change and grow, we must embrace the awkwardness of the newbie. Once we reach cool kid status, it's time

---

351  The Nobel Prize. "Albert Schweitzer – Biographical." NobelPrize.org. Accessed August 18, 2020.

352  Philosoblog, "At Times Our Own Light Goes Out and is Rekindled by a Spark from Another Person," January 14, 2013, accessed September 14, 2020.

to move on. The comfort of knowing everything in life is the beginning of decay. Growth requires us to leave the safe in search of the new.

The next phase of your leadership journey starts with the core of who you are: your identity. Who you are, what you value, and your gifts and talents make up your identity. It's your superpower. Use it to change the world!

# APPENDIX

---

## INTRODUCTION

- Beer, Michael, Magnus Finnström, and Derek Schrader. "Why Leadership Training Fails—and What to Do About It." *Harvard Business Review* (October 2016): 50-57. https://hbr.org/2016/10/why-leadership-training-fails-and-what-to-do-about-it.

- Brown Judy. *The Art and Spirit of Leadership*. Middletown, DE: Trafford Publishing, 2012.

- Carter, Nancy M., Christine Silva. "Mentoring: Necessary But Insufficient for Advancement." Catalyst. Accessed May 23, 2020. https://www.catalyst.org/wp-content/uploads/2019/01/Mentoring_Necessary_But_Insufficient_for_Advancement_Final_120610.pdf.

- Catalyst. "Quick Take: Women of Color in the United States." March 19, 2020 Accessed May 23, 2020. https://www.catalyst.org/research/women-of-color-in-the-united-states/.

- Hougaard, Rasmus. "The Real Crisis In Leadership." *Leadership Strategy* (blog). *Forbes*. September 9, 2018. https://www.forbes.com/sites/rasmushougaard/2018/09/09/the-real-crisis-in-leadership/#6a7e12f3ee47.

- Thomas, Rachel, Marianne Cooper, Ellen Konar, Ali Bohrer, Ava Mohsenin, Lareina Yee, Alexis Krivkovich, Irina Starikova, Jess Huang, and Delia Zanoschi. "Women In The Workplace 2019." McKinsey & Company and LeanIn.Org. https://www.mckinsey.com/featured-insights/gender-equality/women-in-the-workplace-2019.

## CHAPTER 1—THE JOURNEY TO LEADERSHIP

- Allen, George, W. Mark Moore, Lynette Moser, Kathryn Neill, Usha Sambamoorthi, Hershey Bell. "The Role of Servant Leadership and Transformational Leadership in Academic Pharmacy." *American Journal of Pharmaceutical Education* 80 no.7 (2016): 113.

- Bass, Bernard. (1990). "From Transactional to Transformational Leadership: Learning to Share the Vision. *Organizational Dynamics 18* no. 8 (1980): 19-31.

- Biography. "Arthur Ashe Biography." Last modified June 29, 2020. https://www.biography.com/athlete/arthur-ashe.

- Bennis, Warren G. *On Becoming a Leader*. New York: Basic Books, 2009.

- Burns, James. *Leadership*. New York: Harper & Row, 1978.

- Campbell, Joseph. *The Hero with a Thousand Faces*. Princeton: Princeton University Press, 2004.

- Cain, Susan. *Quiet: The Power of Introverts in a World That Can't Stop Talking*. New York: Broadway Books, 2013.

- Carlyle, Thomas. *On Heroes, Hero-worship and the Heroic in History*. London: Chapman and Hall, 1841.

- Cherry, Kendra. "The Eight Major Theories of Leadership." Accessed May 17, 2020. https://www.verywellmind.com/leadership-theories-2795323.

- Early, Gene. "A Short History of Leadership Theories." Accessed May 14, 2020. https://leadersquest.org/content/documents/A_short_history_of_leadership_theories.pdf

- Encyclopedia Brittanica. "Rensis Likert." Accessed May 17, 2020. https://www.britannica.com/biography/Rensis-Likert.

- Frick, Don M. "Robert K. Greenleaf: A Short Biography." Robert K. Greenleaf Center for Servant Leadership. Accessed August 24, 2020. https://www.greenleaf.org/about-us/robert-k-greenleaf-biography/.

- Goleman, Daniel, Richard Boyatzis, and Annie McKee, *Primal Leadership: Realizing the Power of Emotional Intelligence*. Boston: Harvard Business School Press, 2002.

- Greenleaf, Robert K. *Servant Leadership: A Journey into the Nature of Legitimate Power and Greatness*. New York: Paulist Press, 1991.

- Langley, Noel, Judy Garland, Frank Morgan, Mervyn LeRoy, Florence Ryerson, Jack Haley, Ray Bolger, Victor Fleming, Edgar A. Woolf, Bert Lahr, and L. Frank Baum. *The Wizard of Oz*. DVD. Hollywood, CA: Metro Goldwyn Mayer, 1939.

- Library of Congress. "The Wizard of Oz: An American Fairy Tale - To See the Wizard Oz on Stage and Film." December 15, 2010. https://www.loc.gov/exhibits/oz/ozsect2.html.

- MarieCurie. "Marie Curie the Scientist." Accessed August 18, 2020. https://www.mariecurie.org.uk/who/our-history/marie-curie-the-scientist.

- Nobel Prize. "Marie Curie – Biographical." NobelPrize.org. Accessed August 18, 2020. https://www.nobelprize.org/prizes/physics/1903/marie-curie/biographical/.

- Stogdill, Ralph. "Personal Factors Associated with Leadership: A Survey of the Literature." *Journal of Psychology* no. 25 (1948): 35–71.

## CHAPTER 2—THE ROOTS OF LEADERSHIP

- Burns, Ursula. "Ursula Burns Inspires." Lecture at Carnegie Mellon University Tepper School of Business, Pittsburg, PA, October 14, 2019. https://www.youtube.com/watch?v=2lTPh-HOask4&feature=youtu.be.

- Hoyt, Crystal. "Women, Men, and Leadership: Exploring the Gender Gap at the Top." *Social and Personality Psychology Compass* no. 4 (July 2010):484 - 498.

- Goleman, Daniel, Richard Boyatzis, and Annie McKee. Primal *Leadership: Learning to Lead With Emotional Intelligence.* Boston, MA: Harvard Business School Press, 2004.

- Chang, Rachel. "19 Inspirational Maya Angelou Quotes." Biography, January 31, 2020. Accessed August 24, 2020. https:// www.biography.com/news/maya-angelou-quotes.

- Goleman, Daniel (@DanielGolemanEI). "Top 5 amygdala triggers in the workplace: lack of respect, unfair treatment, being unappreciated, not being heard, unrealistic deadlines." Twitter, December 15, 2016, 10:13 a.m. https://twitter.com/danielgolemanei/status/809416053386264576?lang=en.

- Goleman, Daniel. *Emotional Intelligence: Why It Can Matter More Than IQ.* New York: Bantam Books, 1995.

- Heifetz, Ronald, Alexander Grashow, and Martin Linsky. *The Practice of Adaptive Leadership: Tools and Tactics for Changing Your Organization and the World.* Boston, MA: Harvard Business Press, 2009.

- Heifetz, Ronald and Marty Linsky. "A Survival Guide for Leaders." *Harvard Business Review* 80 no. 6 (2002): 65-74. https:// hbr.org/2002/06/a-survival-guide-for-leaders.

- LeanIn. "Ursula Burns." Stories. Accessed October 5, 2020. https://leanin.org/stories/ursula-burns.

- Leslie, Jean and Michael Peterson. *The Benchmarks Sourcebook Three Decades of Related Research.* Greensboro, NC: CCL Press, 2011.

- Mayer, John, Peter Salovey, and David R. Caruso. "Emotional Intelligence." *American Psychologist* 503 (September 2008): 503-517.

- Salovey, Peter and John D. Mayer. "Emotional Intelligence." *Imagination, Cognition and Personality* 9, no. 3 (March 1990): 185–211.

- TalentSmart. "About Emotional Intelligence." Accessed June 10, 2020. https://www.talentsmart.com.

- Yakowicz, Will. "Lessons from Leadership Guru Warren Bennis." *Inc.*, August 4, 2014. Accessed June 10, 2020. https://www.inc.com/will-yakowicz/7-leadership-lessons-from-late-warren-bennis.html.

## CHAPTER 3—YOUR BRAIN ON LEADERSHIP

- Aurelius, Marcus and Gregory Hays. *Meditations.* New York: Modern Library, 2002.

- Belmi, Peter, Rodolfo Cortes Barragan, Margaret A. Neale, and Geoffrey L. Cohen. "Threats to Social Identity Can Trigger Social Deviance." *Personality and Social Psychology Bulletin* 41 no. 4 (April 2015): 467–84.

- Cahalan, Susannah. *Brain On Fire: My Month of Madness.* New York: Simon & Schuster, 2012.

- Cuncic, Arlin. "Amygdala Hijack and the Fight or Flight Response." *Emotions* (blog). *Verywell Mind,* June 16, 2020.

https://www.verywellmind.com/what-happens-during-an-amygdala-hijack-4165944.

- Diamond, Adele. "Executive functions." *Annual Review of Psychology* 64 (2013): 135-68.

- Edinger, Scott. "Three Ways Leaders Make Emotional Connections." *Harvard Business Review* (2012). https://hbr.org/2012/10/three-ways-leaders-make-an-emo.

- Eisenberger, Naomi, Matthew Lieberman, and Kipling Williams. "Does Rejection Hurt? An fMRI Study of Social Exclusion." *Science 302* no.5643 (November 2003): 290-292.

- Goleman, Daniel. *Emotional Intelligence: Why It Can Matter More Than IQ*. New York: Bantam Books, 1995.

- Goleman, Daniel. "The Battle of the Brain". *On Talent and Leadership. Briefings Magazine.* Accessed August 25, 2020. https://www.kornferry.com/insights/articles/the-battle-of-the-brain.

- Hani, Julie. "The Neuroscience of Behavior Change." *Improving Health Outcomes* (blog). *Cecelia Health Marketing,* April 18, 2019. https://www.ceceliahealth.com/blog/2017/6/26/the-neuroscience-of-behavior-change.

- Hanson, Rick. *Hardwiring Happiness: The New Brain Science of Contentment, Calm, and Confidence*. Westminister, MD: Random House, 2013.

- Hanson, Rick and Richard Mendius. *Buddha's Brain: The Practical Neuroscience of Happiness Love & Wisdom.* Oakland, CA: New Harbinger Publications, 2009.

- Kiefer, Tobias. "Neuroleadership – Making Change Happen." *Leadership* (blog). *Ivey Business Journal,* May/June 2011. https://iveybusinessjournal.com/publication/neuroleadership-making-change-happen.

- Komnios, Andreas. "The Concept of the 'Triune Brain'." Interaction Design Foundation. Accessed June 23, 2020. https://www.interaction-design.org/literature/article/the-concept-of-the-triune-brain#:~:text=However%2C%20while%20this%20model%20is,brain%20(Gould%2C%202003).

- LeDoux, Joseph. "The Amygdala." *Current Biology* 17 no. 20 (2007): 868-74.

- Mayfield Clinic. "Anatomy of the Brain." Accessed June 23, 2020. https://d3djccaurgtij4.cloudfront.net/pe-anatomybrain.pdf.

- Nadler, Relly. "Where Did My IQ Points Go?" *Leading with Emotional Intelligence* (blog). *Psychology Today,* April 29, 2011. https://www.psychologytoday.com/us/blog/leading-emotional-intelligence/201104/where-did-my-iq-points-go.

- Newman, John and James Harris. (2009). "The Scientific Contributions of Paul D. MacLean (1913–2007)." *Journal of Nervous and Mental Disease* 197 (2009): 3-5.

- Rock, David. "The Neuroscience of Leadership." *Your Brain at Work* (blog). *Psychology Today.* March 10, 2011. https://www.psychologytoday.com/us/blog/your-brain-work/201103/the-neuroscience-leadership.

- Rock, David. *Your Brain at Work: Strategies for Overcoming Distraction, Regaining Focus, and Working Smarter All Day Long.* New York: Harper Business, 2020.

- Smith, Emily Esfahani. "Social Connection Makes a Better Brain." *The Atlantic,* October 29, 2013. Accessed June 24, 2020. https://www.theatlantic.com/health/archive/2013/10/social-connection-makes-a-better-brain/280934/?utm_source=share&utm_campaign=share.

- *TED.* "Matthew Lieberman: The Social Brain and Its Superpowers." October 7, 2013. Video, 6:23. https://www.youtube.com/watch?v=NNhk3owF7RQ.

- Selig, Meg. "25 Fun and Helpful Quotations About the Human Mind." *Changepower* (blog). *Psychology Today,* November 17, 2016. https://thriveglobal.com/stories/some-more-buddha-quotes-to-rejuvenate-you-with-positivity.

- Sirois, Fushia and Timothy Pychyl. (2013). "Procrastination and the Priority of Short-term Mood Regulation: Consequences for Future Self. *Social and Personality Psychology Compass 7* no.2 (2013): 115–127.

- Van der Kolk, Bessel. *The Body Keeps the Score: Brain, Mind, and Body in the Healing of Trauma.* New York: Viking, 2014.

- Ware, Deann. "Neurons that Fire Together Wire Together–But Why? Hebb's Rule and Synaptic Plasticity." *Awareness* (blog). http://www.awarefulness.com/neurons-that-fire-together-wire-together-but-why-hebbs-rule-and-synaptic-plasticity.

- Winfrey, Oprah. "Remembering Mike Tyson's Apology to Evander Holyfield." June 27, 2016. YouTube video, 3:18. https://www.youtube.com/watch?v=11wLPPTYC30.

## CHAPTER 4—THE CHEMICAL COCKTAIL OF TRUST AND BELONGING

- Boyatzis, Richard and Annie McKee. *Resonant Leadership: Renewing Yourself and Connecting With Others Through Mindfulness, Hope, and Compassion.* Boston: Harvard Business School Press, 2005.

- Brown, Brené, *Braving the Wilderness: The Quest for True Belonging and the Courage to Stand Alone.* New York: Random House, 2017.

- Brown, Brené. *The Gifts of Imperfection: Let Go of Who You Think You're Supposed to Be and Embrace Who You Are.* Center City, MN: Hazelden Publishing, 2010.

- Center for Talent Innovation. "Power of Belonging: What It Is and Why It Matters in Today's Workplace." Accessed July 2, 2020. https://www.talentinnovation.org/publication.cfm?-publication=1660.

- Cigna. "2018 Cigna Loneliness Index." Accessed July 2, 2020. https://www.cigna.com/newsroom/news-releases/2018/

new-cigna-study-reveals-loneliness-at-epidemic-levels-in-america.

- Glaser, Judith E. *Conversational Intelligence: How Great Leaders Build Trust and Get Extraordinary Results.* Brookline, MA: Bibliomotion, Inc, 2014.

- The CreatingWE® Institute. "C-IQ Certification." Accessed July 3, 2020. https://creatingwe.com/services/c-iq-certification.

- Twaronite, Karyn. "Five Findings on the Importance of Belonging," Accessed July 2, 2020. https://www.ey.com/en_us/diversity-inclusiveness/ey-belonging-barometer-workplace-study.

- Twaronite, Karyn. "The Surprising Power of Simply Asking Coworkers How They're Doing." *Harvard Business Review* (February 2019). https://hbr.org/2019/02/the-surprising-power-of-simply-asking-coworkers-how-theyre-doing.

- Whyte, David. *Crossing the Unknown Sea.* New York: Penguin Group, 2002).

- Willis, Janine and Alexander Todorov. "First Impressions: Making Up Your Mind After a 100-MS Exposure to a Face." *Psychological Science* 17 no. 7 (2006): 592-8.

- Zak, Paul J. "The Neuroscience of High-Trust Organizations." *Consulting Psychology Journal: Practice and Research* 70, no. 1, (2018): 45–58.

- Zak, Paul J. "The Neuroscience of Trust." *Harvard Business Review* (January – February 2017): 84 – 90. https://hbr.org/2017/01/the-neuroscience-of-trust.

- Zak, Paul J. "Why Inspiring Stories Make Us React: The Neuroscience of Narrative." *Cerebrum: The Dana Forum On Brain Science* 2015, no. 2 (February 2015).

## CHAPTER 5—EMBRACING YOUR IMPERFECTIONS

- Brach, Tara. "Allow Life to Be Just As It Is: Interview with Clementine Van Wijngaarden." Accessed September 3, 2020. https://www.tarabrach.com/wp-content/uploads/pdf/Flow_Mindfulness-Interview_Tara_Brach.pdf.

- Brach, Tara. "Attend and Befriend: Healing the Fear Body." Streamed on May 28, 2012. Video, 1:00.26. https://www.youtube.com/watch?v=k5w4Mh28wn4.

- Sounds True. "Waking Up from the Trance of Unworthiness with Tara Brach." Streamed on May 22, 2019. Video, 31:33. https://www.youtube.com/watch?v=yoG_kS6XIEE.

- Brach, Tara. *Radical Acceptance: Embracing Your Life with the Heart of a Buddha*. New York: Bantam Books, 2004.

- DeAngelis, Tori. "A Blend of Buddhism and Psychology." Monitor on Psychology. February 2014. https://www.apa.org/monitor/2014/02/buddhism-psychology.

- Economy, Peter. "17 Wise Nelson Mandela Quotes That Will Inspire Your Success." Accessed July 3, 2020. https://www.inc.

com/peter-economy/17-wise-nelson-mandela-quotes-that-will-inspire-your-success.html.

- Firestone, Lisa. "4 Ways to Overcome Your Inner Critic." *Compassion Matters* (blog), *Psychology Today*, May 14, 2013. https://www.psychologytoday.com/us/blog/compassion-matters/201305/4-ways-overcome-your-inner-critic.

- Harter, Jim. "Historic Drop in Employee Engagement Follows Record Rise," Gallup, July 2, 2020. Accessed September 3, 2020. https://www.gallup.com/workplace/313313/historic-drop-employee-engagement-follows-record-rise.aspx.

- L'Engle, Madeleine. *Walking On Water: Reflections on Faith & Art.* Wheaton, IL: H. Shaw, 1980.

- Niedenthal, Paula. "Embodying Emotion," Science 316 no. 582718 (May 2007): 1002-1005. https://science.sciencemag.org/content/316/5827/1002.

- Seppälä, Emma. "What Bosses Gain by Being Vulnerable." *Harvard Business Review*, December 11, 2014. https://hbr.org/2014/12/what-bosses-gain-by-being-vulnerable.

## CHAPTER 6—INCLUSIVE LEADERSHIP

- Bergonzi, Chris. "Understanding Bias and the Brain - Exploring the Neural Pathways of Prejudice May Offer Clues to Lessening Its Effect.' Korn Ferry Institute. Accessed July 6, 2020. https://www.kornferry.com/insights/articles/understanding-bias-and-brain.121.

- Catalyst. "Quick Take: Women of Color in the United States." Research. Accessed March 23, 2020. https://www.catalyst.org/research/women-of-color-in-the-united-states.

- CBS This Morning. "You Don't Have to be a Bigot to Have Bias." March 25, 2019. Video, 6:26. https://www.youtube.com/watch?v=iSyMRAdZXGA.

- Chang, Ailsa. "Jennifer Eberhardt: Can We Overcome Racial Bias? 'Biased' Author Says To Start By Acknowledging It." *NPR*, March 28, 2019. Podcast, 7:48. https://www.npr.org/2019/03/28/705113639/can-we-overcome-racial-bias-biased-author-says-to-start-by-acknowledging-it.

- Desvaux, Georges, Sandrine Devillard, Alix de Zelicourt, Cecile Kossoff, Eric Labaye, and Sandra Sancier-Sultan. "Women Matter 2017." McKinsey & Company, 2017. https://www.mckinsey.com/featured-insights/gender-equality/women-matter-ten-years-of-insights-on-gender-diversity.

- Eberhardt, Jennifer. *Biased: Uncovering the Hidden Prejudice That Shapes What We See, Think, and Do.* New York: Viking, 2019.

- Huang, Jess, Alexis Krivkovich, Irina Starikova, Lareina Yee, and Delia Zanoschi. "Women in the Workplace 2019." LeanIn, McKinsey & Company, October 2019. https://www.mckinsey.com/~/media/McKinsey/Featured%20Insights/Gender%20Equality/Women%20in%20the%20Workplace%202019/Women-in-the-workplace-2019.pdf.

- Hunt, Vivian, Sara Prince, Sundiatu Dixon-Fyle, and Lareina Yee. "Delivering Diversity." McKinsey & Company, 2018. https://www.mckinsey.com/~/media/mckinsey/business%20 functions/organization/our%20insights/delivering%20 through%20diversity/delivering-through-diversity_full-report.ashx.

- Lippmann, Walter. *Public Opinion.* New York: Harcourt, Brace and Company, 1922.

- Palmer, Parker. *The Courage to Teach: Exploring the Inner Landscape of a Teacher's Life.* San Francisco, CA: Jossey-Bass, 1998.

- Ressner, Jeffrey. "Michelle Obama Thesis Was on Racial Divide." *Politico,* February 23, 2008. Accessed September 4, 2020. https://www.politico.com/story/2008/02/michelle-obama-thesis-was-on-racial-divide-008642.

- SpectraDiversity. "Brain Stuff: The Neuroscience Behind Implicit Bias." December 27, 2017. Accessed July 6, 2020. https:// www.spectradiversity.com/2017/12/27/unconscious-bias.

- Travis, Dnika J., Jennifer Thorpe-Moscon, and Courtney McCluney. "Emotional Tax: How Black Women and Men Pay More at Work and How Leaders Can Take Action." Catalyst, 2016. https://www.catalyst.org/research/emotional-tax-how-black-women-and-men-pay-more-at-work-and-how-leaders-can-take-action.

## CHAPTER 7—THE CHANGING FACE OF LEADERSHIP

- American Sociological Association. "Race and Ethnicity." Accessed July 18, 2020. https://www.asanet.org/topics/race-and-ethnicity.

- Brown, Anna. "The Changing Categories the U.S. Census Has Used to Measure Race." Pew Research Center, February 25, 2020. Accessed July 11, 2020. https://www.pewresearch.org/fact-tank/2020/02/25/the-changing-categories-the-u-s-has-used-to-measure-race.

- Catalyst. "Women of Color in the United States." Quick Take, March 19, 2020. https://www.catalyst.org/research/women-of-color-in-the-united-states.

- Cherry, Kendra. "What Does the Acronym BIPOC Mean?", *Race and Identity* (blog), *Very Well Mind*, June 24, 2020. https://www.verywellmind.com/what-is-bipoc-5025158.

- Clair, Judith A., Beth K. Humberd, Elizabeth D. Rouse, and Elise B. Jones. "Loosening Categorical Thinking: Extending the Terrain of Theory and Research on Demographic Identities in Organizations." *Academy of Management Review 44* no. 3 (July 9, 2019): 592–617.

- Cornell, Stephen and Douglas Hartmann. *Ethnicity and Race: Making Identities in a Changing World.* Thousand Oaks, CA: Pine Forge Press, 2007.

- Deloitte. "2018 Deloitte Millennial Survey." Accessed July 11, 2020. https://www2.deloitte.com/tr/en/pages/about-deloitte/articles/millennialsurvey-2018.html.

- Dimock, Michael. "Defining Generations: Where Millennials End and Generation Z Begins." Pew Research Center, January 17, 2019. Accessed July 11, 2020. https://www.pewresearch.org/fact-tank/2019/01/17/where-millennials-end-and-generation-z-begins.

- Frey, William. *Diversity Explosion: How New Racial Demographics Are Remaking America*. Washington, D.C: Brookings Institution Press, 2018.

- Human Rights Campaign (@HRC). "HRC is the nation's largest LGBTQ civil rights organization." Twitter, October 28, 2020, 3:40 pm. https://twitter.com/hrc?lang=en.

- Human Rights Campaign."Pronouns 101." Accessed July 11, 2020. https://assets2.hrc.org/files/assets/resources/HRC_ACAF_Pronouns_101_.pdf.

- Human Rights Campaign. "Talking About Pronouns in the Workplace." Accessed July 11, 2020. https://www.hrc.org/resources/talking-about-pronouns-in-the-workplace.

- Humberd, Beth K., Judy Clair, and Elizabeth (Bess) Rouse. "Employee Demographics Don't Have to Be at Odds with Employees' Identities." *Harvard Business Review*, January 24, 2020. https://hbr.org/2020/01/employee-demographics-dont-have-to-be-at-odds-with-employees-identities.

- Kozuch, Elliott. "Startling Data Reveals Half of LGBTQ Employees in the U.S. Remain Closeted at Work." Human Rights Campaign. Accessed July 11, 2020. https://www.hrc.org/news/hrc-report-startling-data-reveals-half-of-lgbtq-employees-in-us-remain-clos.

- Krogstad, Jens Manuel. "A View of the Nation's Future Through Kindergarten Demographics." Pew Research Center, July 21, 2019. Accessed July 11, 2020. https://www.pewresearch.org/fact-tank/2019/07/31/kindergarten-demographics-in-us.

- Miller, Claire Cain, Kevin Quealy, and Margot Sanger-Katz. "The Top Jobs Where Women Are Outnumbered by Men Named John." *The New York Times*, April 24. 2018. https://www.nytimes.com/interactive/2018/04/24/upshot/women-and-men-named-john.html.

- MK Gandhi Foundation. "Civilization and Culture." Accessed July 11, 2020. https://www.mkgandhi.org/voiceoftruth/civilizationandculture.htm.

- Obama, Barak. "Barack Obama's Feb. 5 Speech." *New York Times*, February 5, 2008. https://www.nytimes.com/2008/02/05/us/politics/05text-obama.html.

- Omi, Michael and Howard Winant. *Racial Formation in the United States*. New York: Routledge, 2015.

- Parker, Kim and Ruth Igielnik. "On the Cusp of Adulthood and Facing an Uncertain Future: What We Know About Gen Z So Far." Pew Research Center, May 14, 2020. Accessed July 11, 2020. https://www.pewsocialtrends.org/essay/on-the-cusp-of-adulthood-and-facing-an-uncertain-future-what-we-know-about-gen-z-so-far.

- Terry, Ruth. "Travel is Said to Increase Cultural Understanding - Does it?" *National Geographic*, July 13, 2020. https://www.nationalgeographic.com/travel/2020/07/does-travel-real-

ly-lead-to empathy/#:~:text=And%20can%20travel%20help%20
facilitate%20this%20learning%3F&text=And%20in%20a%20
2010%20study,and%20associations%E2%80%9D%20with%-
20other%20cultures.

- U.S. Census Bureau. "About Race." Race. Accessed July 11, 2020. https://www.census.gov/topics/population/race/about.html.

- U.S. Census Bureau. "The Changing Economics and Demographics of Young Adulthood: 1975–2016." Accessed July 11, 2020. https://www.census.gov/content/dam/Census/library/publications/2017/demo/p20-579.pdf.

- U.S. Census Bureau. "Projected Race and Hispanic Origin: Main Projections Series for the United States, 2017-2060." Population Division, Washington, DC. Accessed July 11, 2020. https://www.census.gov/content/dam/Census/library/publications/2015/demo/p25-1143.pdf.

- Wong, Curtis M. "New Land O'Lakes CEO Is First Openly Gay Woman To Head A Fortune 500 Company." *Huffington Post*, July 30, 2018. Accessed July 11, 2020. https://www.huffpost.com/entry/beth-ford-land-olakes-gay-ceo_n_5b5f3004e4b-0de86f49966d5.

- Zimmermann, Kim Ann. "What Is Culture?" American Sociological Association. *LiveScience*, July 13, 2017. Accessed July 18, 2020. https://www.livescience.com/21478-what-is-culture-definition-of-culture.html.

## CHAPTER 8—THE UNEVEN PLAYING FIELD

- American University. "About Key: Key Executive Leadership Programs." Accessed September 20, 2020. https://www.american.edu/spa/key.

- Anderson, Rania. "5 Examples of Microaggressions in the Workplace." The Way Women Work. Accessed September 20, 2020. https://thewaywomenwork.com/2019/04/5-examples-of-microaggressions-in-the-workplace.

- Block, Caryn, Sandy Koch, Benjamin Liberman, Tarani Merriweather, and Loriann Roberson. "Contending with Stereotype Threat at Work: A Model of Long-Term Responses 1Ψ7." *The Counseling Psychologist* 39, no. 4 (May 2011): 570-600.

- Brookings Institution. "WashU at Brookings." LEGIS Congressional Fellowship. Accessed September 20, 2020. https://www.brookings.edu/fellowships-programs/legis.

- Catalyst. "Women of Color in the United States." Quick Take, March 19, 2020. Accessed July 23, 2020. https://www.catalyst.org/research/women-of-color-in-the-united-states.

- CBS This Morning. "CEO Mellody Hobson on Race in Corporate America and How to Create Change." June 24, 2020. Video, 5:28. Accessed July 26, 2020. https://www.cbsnews.com/video/ceo-mellody-hobson-on-race-in-corporate-america-and-how-to-create-change.

- DeAngelis, Tori. "Unmasking 'Racial Micro Aggressions'." *American Psychological Association Monitor* 40 no. 2 (February 2009): 42. https://www.apa.org/monitor/2009/02/micro-aggression.

- Dovidio, John and Samuel Gaertner. "Aversive Racism and Selection Decisions: 1989 and 1999." *Psychological Science* 11, no. 4 (July 2000): 315–319.

- Dovidio, John, Samuel Gaertner, Kerry Kawakami, and Gordon Hodson. (2002). "Why Can't We Just Get Along? Interpersonal Biases and Interracial Distrust." *Cultural Diversity and Ethnic Minority Psychology* no. 8 (2002): 88-102.

- Ellison, Ralph. *Invisible Man*. New York: Vintage International, 1995.

- Grandin, Greg. "Obama, Melville, and the Tea Party." *The New York Times*, January 18, 2014. https://www.nytimes.com/2014/01/19/opinion/sunday/obama-melville-and-the-tea-party.html.

- Hobson, Mellody. "Color Blind or Color Brave?" *TED*, May 5, 2014. Video, 14:14. https://www.youtube.com/watch?v=oK-tALHe3Y9Q.

- Holder, Aisha, Margo Jackson, and Joseph Ponterotto. "Racial Microaggression Experiences and Coping Strategies of Black Women in Corporate Leadership." *Qualitative Psychology,* 2 no.2, (2015).

- Kurian, Brian. "Shining A Light On Racism," *Medium*, April, 20, 2019. Accessed October 4, 2020. https://medium.com/@brian.kurian/shining-a-light-on-racism-f1587a1db311.

- LeanIn.Org and McKinsey & Company. "Women in the Workplace 2018." Accessed September 2, 2020. https://womenintheworkplace.com.

- McLean, Bethany. "Why Sheryl Sandberg, Bill Bradley, and Oprah Love Mellody Hobson." *Vanity Fair Magazine,* March 30, 2015. Accessed July 25, 2020. https://www.vanityfair.com/news/2015/03/mellody-hobson-ariel-investments-fighting-stereotype.

- Nadal, Kevin. "A Guide to Responding to Microaggressions." CUNY Forum. Accessed July 25, 2020. https://advancingjustice-la.org/sites/default/files/ELAMICRO%20A_Guide_to_Responding_to_Microaggressions.pdf.

- Purdie-Vaughns, Valerie and Richard Eibach. "Intersectional Invisibility: The Distinctive Advantages and Disadvantages of Multiple Subordinate-Group Identities." *Sex Roles* no. 59 (2008): 377–391.

- Rosette. Ashleigh and Robert Livingston. "Failure is Not an Option for Black Women: Effects of Organizational Performance on Leaders with Single Versus Dual-Subordinate Identities." *Journal of Experimental Social Psychology* 48, no. 5 (2012): 1162-1167.

- Sesko, Amanda and Monica Biernat. "Invisibility of Black Women: Drawing Attention to Individuality." *Group Processes & Intergroup Relations* 21, no. 1 (January 2018): 141–58.

- Sesko, Amanda and Monica Biernat. "Prototypes of Race and Gender: The Invisibility of Black Women." *Journal of Experimental Social Psychology,* 46 no.2 (2010), 356–360.

- Smith, Alexis. "Interviews with 59 Black Female Executives Explore Intersectional Invisibility and Strategies to Overcome It." *Harvard Business Review,* May 10, 2018.https://hbr. org/2018/05/interviews-with-59-black-female-executives-explore-intersectional-invisibility-and-strategies-to-overcome-it.

- Smith, Anna. "What to Know About Microaggressions." *Medical News Today,* June 11, 2020. Accessed July 25, 2020.https:// www.medicalnewstoday.com/articles/microagressions#types.

- Steele, Claude and Joshua Aronson. "Stereotype Threat and the Intellectual Test Performance of African-Americans." *Journal of Personality and Social Psychology* 62 no.1 (1995): 26-37.

- Sue, Derald, Christina Capodilupo, Gina Torino, Jennifer Bucceri, Aisha Holder, Kevin Nadal, and Marta Esquilin. "Racial Microaggressions in Everyday Life: Implications for Clinical Practice." *The American Psychologist* 62 no. 4 (2007): 271-286.

## CHAPTER 9—THE INTERSECTION OF LEADERSHIP AND IDENTITY

- Brah, Avtar and Ann Phoenix. "Ain't I A Woman? Revisiting Intersectionality." *Journal of International Women's Studies* 5 vol. 3 (2004): 75-86. https://www.researchgate.net/publication/228698804_Ain't_IA_Woman_Revisiting_Intersectionality.

- Crenshaw, Kimberlé. "The Urgency of Intersectionality | Kimberlé Crenshaw." *TED*, December 7, 2016. Video, 18:49. https://www.ted.com/talks/kimberle_crenshaw_the_urgency_of_intersectionality?language=en.

- Demby, Gene. "How Code-Switching Explains The World." *Code Switch* (blog). *NPR*, April 8, 2013.mhttps://www.npr.org/sections/codeswitch/2013/04/08/176064688/how-code-switching-explains-the-world.

- *Encyclopaedia Britannica Online*. "Code-Switching." By Carlos D. Morrison. Accessed July 11, 2020. https://www.britannica.com/topic/code-switching.

- *Encyclopaedia Britannica Online*. "Ebonics." By Salikoko Sangol Mufwene. Accessed July 11, 2020. https://www.britannica.com/topic/Ebonics.

- Gelles, David. "Stacy Brown-Philpot of TaskRabbit on Being a Black Woman in Silicon Valley." *New York Times*, July 13, 2018. https://www.nytimes.com/2018/07/13/business/stacy-brown-philpot-taskrabbit-corner-office.html.

- Graham, Steadman. *Identity Leadership*. New York: Center Street, 2019.

- Guynn, Jessica. "TaskRabbit Teams with Black Lawmakers to Boost Tech Diversity." *USA Today*, April 23, 2016. https://www.usatoday.com/story/tech/news/2016/04/21/taskrabbit-diversity-inclusion-congressional-black-caucus/83314106.

- Harris, Ida. "Code-Switching Is Not Trying to Fit in to White Culture, It's Surviving It." *Yes Magazine,* December 17, 2019. Accessed July 12, 2020. https://www.yesmagazine.org/opinion/2019/12/17/culture-code-switching.

- Heshmat, Shahram. "What Do We Mean by Identity and Why Does Identity Matter?" *Science of Choice* (blog). *Psychology Today,* December 8, 2014. https://www.psychologytoday.com/us/blog/science-choice/201412/basics-identity.

- Karabel, Shellie. "Dressing Like A Leader: Style Tips For Women In The Spotlight." *Forbes Magazine,* January 16, 2016. Accessed September 20, 2020. https://www.forbes.com/sites/shelliekarabell/2016/01/16/dressing-like-a-leader-style-tips-for-women-in-the-spotlight/#515e9f522466.

- McGirt, Ellen. "Target's Caroline Wanga Is Here to Change the World." *Fortune Magazine,* October 10, 2019. Accessed April 5, 2020. https://fortune.com/2019/10/10/targets-caroline-wanga-is-here-to-change-the-world-raceahead.

- McGirt, Ellen and Jessica Helfand. "S7E1: Caroline Wanga." *The Design of Business | The Business of Design*, October 8, 2019. Podcast, 34:28. https://designobserver.com/feature/s7e1-caroline-wanga/40124.

- McKissack,Pat. *Sojourner Truth: Ain't I a Woman? 1944-2017.* New York: Scholastic, 1992.

- *Merriam-Webster.com Dictionary*, s.v. "Intersectionality." Accessed September 10, 2020. https://www.merriam-webster.com/dictionary/intersectionality.

- Obama, Michelle. *Becoming*. New York: Random House, 2018.

- Perman, Merrill. "The Origin of the Term 'Intersectionality'." *Language Corner* (blog). *Columbia Journalism Review*, October 23, 2018. https://www.cjr.org/language_corner/intersectionality.php.

- Posada, Alondra. "Spanglish is a Language Too: Alondra Posada." *TEDx Talks,* June 27, 2018. Video, 6:16. https://www.ted.com/talks/alondra_posada_spanglish_is_a_language_too.

- Tanenbaum Center for Interreligious Understanding. "2018 Religious Diversity Leadership Summit Bios." Accessed September 20, 2020. https://tanenbaum.org/wp-content/uploads/2018/05/2018-RDLS-Bios.pdf.

- Thomas, Rachel, Marianne Cooper, Ellen Konar, Ali Bohrer, Ava Mohsenin, Lareina Yee, Alexis Krivkovich, Irina Starikova, Jess Huang, and Delia Zanoschi. "Women In The Workplace 2019." McKinsey & Company and LeanIn.Org. https://www.mckinsey.com/featured-insights/gender-equality/women-in-the-workplace-2019.

- Travis, Dnika J., Jennifer Thorpe-Moscon, and Courtney McCluney. "Emotional Tax: How Black Women and Men Pay More at Work and How Leaders Can Take Action." Catalyst, 2016. https://www.catalyst.org/research/emotional-tax-how-black-women-and-men-pay-more-at-work-and-how-leaders-can-take-action.

- Wanga, Caroline. "Authenticity: Who You are is Non-Negotiable," Management Leadership for Tomorrow,

April 29, 2020. Video, 37:16. https://www.youtube.com/
watch?v=HAIiqOG4KBU.

- Wanga, Caroline. "Caroline Wanga, VP Diversity and Inclusion - Target Corporation," The Forum on Workplace Inclusion, May 19, 2016. Video, 3:33. https://www.youtube.com/
watch?v=3Q_WVYVJhZ4.

## CHAPTER 10—OWNING YOUR NARRATIVE

- Bennis, Warren. *On Becoming a Leader.* Cambridge, MA: Perseus Pub, 2003.

- Bennis, Warren and Robert Thomas. "Crucibles of Leadership."
*Harvard Business Review* (September 2002):39-45. https://hbr.
org/2002/09/crucibles-of-leadership.

- Bentley, Sarah, Katherine Greenaway, S. Alexander Haslam,
Tegan Cruwys, Niklas Steffens, Catherine Haslam, and Ben
Cull. "Social Identity Mapping Online. *Journal of Personality
and Social Psychology* 118 no. 2 (2020): 213–241.

- Boyatzis, Richard, Kylie Rochford, and Scott Taylor. "The
Role of the Positive Emotional Attractor in Vision and Shared
Vision: Toward Effective Leadership, Relationships, and
Engagement." *Frontiers in Psychology* 670 vol. 6 (May 21, 2015).

- Brown, Brené. *Daring Greatly: How the Courage to Be Vulnerable Transforms the Way We Live, Love, Parent and Lead.* New
York: Penguin Random House 2013.

- Brown, Brené, *Rising Strong.* New York: Spiegel & Grau, 2015.

- Covey, Stephen. *The 7 Habits of Highly Effective People: Restoring the Character Ethic*. New York: Free Press, 2004.

- Chiron Strategic LLC. "Bios." Accessed July 13, 2020. https://chironstrategic.com/bios.

- Cruwys, Tegan, Niklas Steffens, S. Alexander Haslam, Catherine Haslam, Joianda Jetten, and Genevieve Dingle. "Social Identity Mapping: A Procedure for Visual Representation and Assessment of Subjective Multiple Group Memberships." *The British Journal of Social Psychology* 55 no. 4 (2016): 613-642.

- ICF Metro DC. "Capital Coaches Conference Agenda." Accessed July 13, 2020. https://icfmetrodc.starchapter.com/images/CCCProgram91219.pdf.

- Klein, Kitty and Adriel Boals. "Expressive Writing Can Increase Working Memory Capacity." *Journal of Experimental Psychology* 130 no.3 (September 2001):520-33.

- Lieberman, Charlotte. "Audre Lorde." Writing on Glass (blog). Accessed July 13, 2020.https://www.writingonglass.com/audre-lorde.

- Tajfel, Henri and John C. Turner. "The Social Identity Theory of Intergroup Behavior." *Political Psychology* (January 9, 2004): 276–293.

- Taranath, Anu. "Difference, Identity and Power." Washington University Office of Minority Affairs. Accessed July12, 2020. https://www.washington.edu/omad/ctcenter/projects-com-

mon-book/mountains-beyond-mountains/difference-identi-
ty-and-power.

- Weinreich, Peter and Wendy Saunderson. *Analysing Identity: Cross-Cultural, Societal, and Clinical Contexts*. London: Routledge, 2003.

- Whyte, David. *Crossing the Unknown Sea: Work As a Pilgrimage of Identity*. New York: Riverhead Books, 2001.

## CHAPTER 11—THE INNER CRITIC

- BBC News. "Shot Pakistan Schoolgirl Malala Yousafzai Addresses UN." July 12, 2014. Accessed March 28, 2020. https://www.bbc.com/news/av/world-23295262.

- Bennett, Jessica. "How to Overcome 'Impostor Syndrome'." *New York Times*. Accessed March 18, 2020. https://www.nytimes.com/guides/working-womans-handbook/overcome-impostor-syndrome.

- Burnett, Jane. "6 Powerful People on How They Manage Their Imposter Syndrome." Thrive Global, December 7, 2018. Accessed July 15, 2020. https://thriveglobal.in/stories/6-powerful-people-on-how-they-manage-their-impostor-syndrome.

- Charles, Ron. "National Book Festival in Washington Breaks Attendance and Sales Records." *Washington Post*, September 3, 2018. Accessed March 23, 2020. https://www.washingtonpost.com/entertainment/books/national-book-festival-in-washington-breaks-attendance-and-sales-records/2018/09/03/f244960a-aeb7-11e8-9a6a-565d92a3585d_story.html.

- Clance, Pauline Rose. "Imposter Phenomenon." Accessed June 23, 2020. https://www.paulineroseclance.com/impostor_phenomenon.html.

- Clance, Pauline and Suzanne Imes. "The Imposter Phenomenon in High Achieving Women: Dynamics and Therapeutic Intervention." *Psychotherapy: Theory, Research & Practice* 15 no.3 (1978): 241–247.

- Cokley, Kevin, LeannSmith, Donte Bernard, Ashley Hurst, Stacey Jackson, Steven Stone, Olufunke Awosogba, Chastity Saucer, Marlon Bailey, and Davia Roberts. "Impostor Feelings as a Moderator and Mediator of the Relationship Between Perceived Discrimination and Mental Health Among Racial/Ethnic Minority College Students." *Journal of Counseling Psychology* vol. 64 no.2 (2017): 141-154.

- Doggett, Jolie. "Imposter Syndrome Hits Harder When You're Black." HuffPost, October 10, 2019. Accessed September 12, 2020. https://www.huffpost.com/entry/imposter-syndrome-racism-discrimination_l_5d9f2c00e4b06ddfc514ec5c.

- Ferrera, America. "My identity is a Superpower - Not an Obstacle | America Ferrera." *TED*, June 21, 2019. Video, 14:02. https://www.ted.com/talks/america_ferrera_my_identity_is_a_superpower_not_an_obstacle?language=en.

- Library of Congress. "About the Librarian." Accessed March 28, 2020. https://www.loc.gov/about/about-the-librarian/#:~:text=Carla%20Hayden%20was%20sworn%20in,U.S.%20Senate%20on%20July%2013.

- Library of Congress. "U.S. Supreme Court Justice Sonia Sotomayor: 2018 National Book Festival." October 18, 2018. Video, 57:44. https://www.loc.gov/item/webcast-8465.

- Malala Fund. "Malala's Story." Accessed March 28, 2020. https://malala.org/malalas-story.

- Miller, Darlene and Signe Kastberg. *"Of Blue Collars and Ivory Towers: Women from Blue-Collar Backgrounds in Higher Education."* Roeper Review 18 no.1(September 1995): 27–33.

- Nobel Prize. "The Nobel Peace Prize for 2014." Accessed March 28, 2020. https://www.nobelprize.org/prizes/peace/2014/summary.

- Mohr, Tara. *Playing Big: Practical Wisdom for Women Who Want to Speak Up, Create, and Lead.* New York: Avery, 2015.

- Sakulku, Jaruwan and James Alexander. "The Imposter Phenomenon." *International Journal of Behavioral Science* 6 no. 1 (2011):73-92.

- Sotomayor, Sonia. "My Beloved World." New York: Random House, 2013.

- SuperPopVIP. "America Ferrera Introduces Malala Yousafzai at Glamour Magazine's 23rd Annual Women of The Year Awards Event at the Carnegie Hall." November 24, 2013. Video, 1:07. https://www.youtube.com/watch?v=22iITOL9I-AQ&t=1s.

- Wong, Kristin. "Dealing with Impostor Syndrome When You're Treated as an Impostor." *New York Times,* June 12, 2018. Accessed March 18, 2020. https://www.nytimes.com/2018/06/12/smarter-living/dealing-with-impostor-syndrome-when-youre-treated-as-an-impostor.html.

- Young, Valerie. *The Secret Thoughts of Successful Women: Why Capable People Suffer from the Impostor Syndrome and How to Thrive in Spite of It.* New York: Crown Business, 2011.

## CHAPTER 12—THE MAKING OF A LEADER

- BBC News. "Maya Angelou: In Her Own Words." May 28, 2014. Accessed March 28, 2020. https://www.bbc.com/news/world-us-canada-27610770#:~:text=%22People%20will%20forget%20what%20you,how%20amazing%20you%20can%20be.%22.

- Bennis, Warren. *On Becoming a Leader.* New York: Basic Books, 2009.

- Bennis, Warren and Robert Thomas. "Crucibles of Leadership." *Harvard Business Review* 80 no. 124 (September 2002): 39-45. https://hbr.org/2002/09/crucibles-of-leadership.

- Campbell, Joseph. *The Hero with a Thousand Faces* Campbell. Princeton, N.J.: Princeton University Press, 2004.

- Campbell, Joseph. *Joseph Campbell and the Power of Myth with Bill Moyers.* Edited by Betty Sue Flowers. New York: Doubleday and Co., 1988.

- McGregor, Jena. "Remembering Leadership Sage Warren Bennis." *Washington Post*, August 4, 2014, On Leadership. https://www.washingtonpost.com/news/on-leadership/wp/2014/08/04/remembering-leadership-sage-warren-bennis.

- Oliver, Mary. *Dream Work*. Boston: Atlantic Monthly Press, 1986.

- Phipps, Wintley. "Wintley Phipps Quotes." Goodreads. Accessed March 28, 2020. https://www.goodreads.com/author/quotes/576174.Wintley_Phipps.

- Star Wars. "A Dummy's Guide to the Star Wars Universe for Those Who Feel the Force." *The Sunday Guardian,* March 10, 2016. Accessed March 26, 2020. https://www.sundayguardianlive.com/movies/2267-dummy-s-guide-star-wars-universe-those-who-feel-force.

- Swatman, Rachel. "1977: Highest-Grossing Sci-F Series at the Box Office." Guinness World Records. August 19, 2015. Accessed July 4, 2020. https://www.guinnessworldrecords.com/news/60at60/2015/8/1977-highest-grossing-sci-fi-series-at-the-box-office-392957.

## CHAPTER 13—AUTHENTIC LEADERSHIP

- Avolio, Bruce and William Gardner. "Authentic Leadership Development: Getting to the Root of Positive Forms of Leadership." *The Leadership Quarterly* 16 no. 3 (May 2005): 315-338.

- Barnes, Melody. "Authentic Leadership as a Woman of Color." *NYU Leads*, May 6, 2016. Video, 5:59. https://www.youtube.com/watch?v=RRktNHhuc6s.

- Breathnach, Sarah Ban. *Simple Abundance: A Daybook of Comfort and Joy.* New York: Warner Books, 1995.

- Buote, Vanessa. "Most Employees Feel Authentic at Work, but It Can Take a While." *Harvard Business Review* (May 11, 2016). https://hbr.org/2016/05/most-employees-feel-authentic-at-work-but-it-can-take-a-while#:~:text=Overall%2C%20 72%25%20of%20people%20said,to%20feel%20comfortable%20 being%20authentic.

- Coelho, Paulo. @paulocoelho. January 20, 2019. Accessed March 28, 2020. https://twitter.com/paulocoelho/status/1087 090821650878464?lang=en.

- Emerson, Ralph Waldo. "Ralph Waldo Emerson Quotes." AZQuotes. Accessed September 13, 2020.https://www.azquotes. com/quote/1277422.

- Fudge, Ann. "Ann Fudge." The HistoryMakers. Accessed September 22, 2020. https://www.thehistorymakers.org/biography/ ann-fudge.

- George, Bill, Peter Sims, Andrew McLean and Diana Mayer. "Discovering Your Authentic Leadership." *Harvard Business Review* (February 2007). https://hbr.org/2007/02/discovering-your-authentic-leadership.

- Hanson, Rick. "Who Is Behind the Mask?" *Your Wise Brain* (blog). *Psychology Today,* March 17, 2011. https://www.psychologytoday.com/us/blog/your-wise-brain/201509/who-is-behind-the-mask.

- Hopkins, Margaret and Deborah O'Neil. "Authentic Leadership: Application to Women Leaders." *Frontiers in Psychology* 6 no. 959 (July 15, 2015).

- Ibarra, Herminia. "The Authenticity Paradox." *Harvard Business Review* (January - February 2015). https://hbr.org/2015/01/the-authenticity-paradox.

- McGirt, Ellen. "The Black Ceiling: Why African-American Women Aren't Making It to the Top in Corporate America." *Fortune Magazine*, September 27, 2017. Accessed September 13, 2020. https://fortune.com/2017/09/27/black-female-ceos-fortune-500-companies.

- McHugh, Caroline. "The Art of Being Yourself." *TEDxTalks*. February 15, 2013. Video, 26:23. https://www.youtube.com/watch?v=veEQQ-N9xWU.

- McHugh, Caroline. *Never Not a Lovely Moon: The Art of Being Yourself.* Wilmington, OH: Orange Frazer Press, 2009.

- Murray, Judy. "A New Start: Judy Murray on the 'Baby Buddhist' Who Cured Her Terror of Public Speaking." *The Guardian*, January 31, 2018. Accessed March 23, 2020. https://www.theguardian.com/lifeandstyle/2018/dec/31/a-new-start-judy-murray-on-the-baby-buddhist-who-cured-her-terror-of-public-speaking.

- Star Trek. "Star Trek: The Original Series." IMDb. Accessed September 22, 2020. https://www.imdb.com/title/tt0060028.

- van den Bosch, Ralph and Toon Taris. "Authenticity at Work: Development and Validation of an Individual Authenticity Measure at Work." *Journal of Happiness* 15 no. 1 (January 2014).

- Walumbwa, Fred, Bruce Avolio, William Gardner, Tara Wernsing, and Suzanne Peterson. "Authentic Leadership: Development and Validation of a Theory-Based Measure." *Journal of Management* 34 no. 1 (February 2008): 89–126.

- Ware, Bronnie. *The Top Five Regrets of the Dying: A Life Transformed By the Dearly Departing.* Carlsbad, CA: Hay House, 2012.

- Winfrey, Oprah. "What Oprah Knows for Sure About Authenticity." *Oprah.com.* Accessed Mar 28, 2020. http://www.oprah.com/spirit/oprah-on-the-importance-of-authenticity-what-i-know-for-sure.

- Wittenberg, Anka. "The Business Impact of Authentic Leadership." *Entrepreneur*, April 20, 2015. https://www.entrepreneur.com/article/245111#:~:text=When%20people%20feel%20free%20to,the%20mission%20of%20the%20enterprise.

## CHAPTER 14—THE THREE C'S OF LEADERSHIP

- Auvinen, Tommi, Pasi Sajasalo, Teppo Sintonen, Kaisa Pekkala, Tuomo Takala, and Vilma Luoma-aho. "Evolution of Strategy Narration and Leadership Work in the Digital Era." *Leadership* 15 no. 2 (April 2019): 205–25.

- Brown, Aaron. "How to Measure Employee Engagement the Right Way." Quantum Workplace, January 21, 2020. Accessed

September 14, 2020. https://www.quantumworkplace.com/future-of-work/the-right-way-to-measure-employee-engagement.

- Brown, H Jackson. "Twenty Years From Now You Will Be More Disappointed By The Things You Didn't Do Than By The Ones You Did Do." Quote Investigator, September 29, 2011. Accessed September 14, 2020. https://quoteinvestigator.com/2011/09/29/you-did.

- Covey, Stephen. *The 7 Habits Of Highly Effective People: Restoring The Character Ethic.* New York: Free Press, 2004.

- Godin, Seth. *Tribes: We Need You to Lead Us.* New York: Penguin Group, 2008.

- Gostick, Adrian and Chester Elton. *Leading with Gratitude: Eight Leadership Practices for Extraordinary Business Results.* New York: Harper Business, 2020.

- Harari, Oren and Ryan Chris. *The Leadership Secrets of Colin Powell.* New York: McGraw-Hill/TDM Audio, 2003.

- Jen, Amy Su. *The Leader You Want to Be: Five Essential Principles for Bringing Out Your Best Self--Every Day.* Boston, MA: Harvard Business Review Press, 2019.

- King, Martin Luther. *Strength to Love.* New York: Harper & Row, 1963.

- *Merriam-Webster.com Dictionary.* s.v. "Legacy." Accessed September 14, 2020. https://www.merriam-webster.com/dictionary/legacy.

- Schweitzer, Albert. "Albert Schweitzer – Biographical." Nobel-Prize.org. The Nobel Prize. Accessed August 18, 2020. https://www.nobelprize.org/prizes/peace/1952/schweitzer/biographical.

- Schweitzer, Albert. "At Times Our Own Light Goes Out and is Rekindled by a Spark from Another Person." Philosoblog, January 14, 2013. Accessed September 14, 2020.https://philosiblog.com/2013/01/14/at-times-our-own-light-goes-out-and-is-rekindled-by-a-spark-from-another-person.

- Sweatt, Lydia. "11 Quotes About Leaving a Legacy." *Success* (blog). Accessed May 28, 2020. https://www.success.com/11-quotes-about-leaving-a-legacy.

- Vanzant, Iyanla. "As you learn to TRUST YOURSELF." @iyanlavanzant. Twitter, September 1, 2013, 10:00 p.m. https://twitter.com/IyanlaVanzant/status/374351113153425408.

- Walker, Alice. "Alice Walker Quotes." BrainyQuote.com. Accessed September 14, 2020.https://www.brainyquote.com/authors/alice-walker-quotes.

- Whyte III, Daniel. *Letters to Young Black Women*. Torch Legacy Publications, 2006.

- Wood, Alex, Stephen Joseph and John Maltby. "Gratitude Uniquely Predicts Satisfaction with Life: Incremental Validity Above the Domains and Facets of the Five Factor Model." *Personality and Individual Differences* 45 no. 1 (2008): 49-54.

- Zemantic, Zac. "Experiencing Spidey-Sense in Spider-Man: The Science Behind Science Fiction." *Down to a Science* (blog). *Connecticut Science Center.* Accessed September 22, 2020. https://ctsciencecenter.org/blog/experiencing-spidey-sense-in-spider-man-the-science-behind-science-fiction.

# ACKNOWLEDGEMENTS

I am blessed to have a family who cheers for me no matter what. This book would not have happened without the love and support of my family and friends. They're the foundation for everything I've accomplished in my life and career.

Thank you to my first teachers—my parents Rufus and Josephine Jefferson. You taught me the most important lessons: faith, family, service to others, and love. In addition to having great parents, I'm fortunate to have an amazing sister and brother, Carla Finney and Eric Jefferson, who are always in my corner. My husband Anthony "Tony" Johnson has encouraged me throughout this journey. His love and support are an amazing gift from God. One of the great blessings of marrying my husband is having Towana Lampkins as my step-daughter and Mary Johnson as my mother-in-law. I'm eternally grateful to my friend Keya Briscoe for always being in my corner.

My gratitude goes out to everyone who generously gave their time and wisdom: Janettarose Greene, Maria DiPasquantonio, Selika Gore, DeShawn Shepard, Traci Mitchell, Heidi

Junk, Kolleen Bouchane, Wendy Moomaw, Wendy Morton-Huddleston, Tanaia Parker, Ruthanne Smith, Wendy Swires, Maria Van Hekken, Chris Wahl, Emilia (Mel) Szarek, Janelle Johnson, Anna Boyd, Deepti Gudipati, LaTonya Mims, and Justine Desmarais. Thank you for sharing your stories, advice, and wise counsel.

Special thanks to David Whatley, Marilyn Jackson-Brame, Gwendolyn Sykes, Anne Ferro, Brodi Fontenot, Sarah Feinberg, Keith Washington, and the late Jerry Ball. I'm grateful to each of you for being great leaders, mentors, and friends.

I wrote this book because my leadership journey has been unique. There were many times when I've been the only person who looked like me, thought like me, or had my background. I hope this book can help you embrace your unique identity as your superpower and use it to guide your leadership journey.

Made in the USA
Middletown, DE
23 December 2020